The Genuine
Oneness
of the Body,
the Proper
One Accord
in the Church,
and the
Direction of
the Lord's
Move Today

The Holy Word for Morning Revival

Witness Lee

Living Stream Ministry
Anaheim, CA • www.lsm.org

First Edition, June 2012.

ISBN 978-0-7363-6245-0

Published by

Living Stream Ministry
2431 W. La Palma Ave., Anaheim, CA 92801 U.S.A.
P. O. Box 2121, Anaheim, CA 92814 U.S.A.

Printed in the United States of America

12 13 14 / 4 3 2 1

2012 Memorial Day Weekend Conference

THE GENUINE ONENESS OF THE BODY, THE PROPER ONE ACCORD IN THE CHURCH, AND THE DIRECTION OF THE LORD'S MOVE TODAY

Contents

Week	*Title*	*Page*
	Preface	v
	General Subject and Banners	1
1	**The Lord's Prayer for the Glorification of the Triune God in the Oneness of the Body of Christ**	
	Outline	2
	Day 1	6
2	**The Oneness of the Body of Christ— the Oneness in the Triune God Typified by the Tabernacle**	
	Outline	20
	Day 1	24
3	**The Vision of the Proper One Accord in the Church**	
	Outline	38
	Day 1	42
4	**The Practice of the Proper One Accord in the Church**	
	Outline	56
	Day 1	60

(primarily responsibility by Santa Clara)

Santa Clara will prep for Labor Day

(gp C , gp E+K)
(15 saints among us pray)

iii

Week	Title	Page
5	**The Lord's Move Today**	
	Outline	74
	Day 1	78
6	**The Direction of the Lord's Move Today**	
	Outline	93
	Day 1	98
	Recovery Version Reading Schedules:	
	Old Testament	114
	New Testament	118
	Daily Verse Cards	123

Preface

1. This book is intended as an aid to believers in developing a daily time of morning revival with the Lord in His word. At the same time, it provides a limited review of the Memorial Day weekend conference held in Bellevue, Washington, May 25-28, 2012. The general subject of the conference was "The Genuine Oneness of the Body, the Proper One Accord in the Church, and the Direction of the Lord's Move Today." Through intimate contact with the Lord in His word, the believers can be constituted with life and truth and thereby equipped to prophesy in the meetings of the church unto the building up of the Body of Christ.

2. The entire content of this book is taken primarily from the published conference outlines, the text and footnotes of the Recovery Version of the Bible, selections from the writings of Witness Lee and Watchman Nee, and *Hymns,* all of which are published by Living Stream Ministry.

3. The book is divided into weeks. One conference message is covered per week. Each week presents first the message outline, followed by six daily portions, a hymn, and then some space for writing. The message outline has been divided into days, corresponding to the six daily portions. Each daily portion covers certain points and begins with a section entitled "Morning Nourishment." This section contains selected verses and a short reading that can provide rich spiritual nourishment through intimate fellowship with the Lord. The "Morning Nourishment" is followed by a section entitled "Today's Reading," a longer portion of ministry related to the day's main points. Each day's portion concludes with a short list of references for further reading and some space for the saints to make notes concerning their spiritual inspiration, enlightenment, and enjoyment to serve as a reminder of what they have received of the Lord that day.

4. The space provided at the end of each week is for composing a short prophecy. This prophecy can be composed by

considering all of our daily notes, the "harvest" of our inspirations during the week, and preparing a main point with some sub-points to be spoken in the church meetings for the organic building up of the Body of Christ.

5. Following the last week in this volume, we have provided reading schedules for both the Old and New Testaments in the Recovery Version with footnotes. These schedules are arranged so that one can read through both the Old and New Testaments of the Recovery Version with footnotes in two years.

6. As a practical aid to the saints' feeding on the Word throughout the day, we have provided verse cards at the end of the volume, which correspond to each day's scripture reading. These may be removed and carried along as a source of spiritual enlightenment and nourishment in the saints' daily lives.

7. The conference message outlines were compiled by Living Stream Ministry from the writings of Witness Lee and Watchman Nee. The outlines, footnotes, and references in the Recovery Version of the Bible are by Witness Lee. All of the other references cited in this publication are from the published ministry of Witness Lee and Watchman Nee.

Memorial Day Weekend Conference

(May 25-28, 2012)

General Subject:

The Genuine Oneness of the Body, the Proper One Accord in the Church, and the Direction of the Lord's Move Today

Banners:

To live and act in the Father's life
with the Father's nature to express the Father
is glory, and it is in this glory that we all are one.

For the Lord's up-to-date move, all the churches
need to be in one accord, having one heart
and one way, learning to be in one spirit
with one soul, and speaking the same thing.

The Lord's move today is for His people
to enter into a new revival through the recovery
of the priesthood of the gospel
in the New Testament for the organic
building up of the church as the Body of Christ.

The direction of the Lord's move today
is to build up the organic Body of Christ
as the organism of the processed and dispensing
Triune God, to prepare the bride
as the counterpart of the Bridegroom, and to
bring in the kingdom of God as the spreading of
the divine life for God's eternal administration.

The Lord's Prayer
for the Glorification of the Triune God
in the Oneness of the Body of Christ

Scripture Reading: John 17:1-24

Day 1
Wann'ly

I. **The Lord's prayer in John 17 was for the glori-fication, the manifestation, the expression, of the Triune God; God's eternal purpose is to manifest, to express, Himself (vv. 1-5; Gen. 1:26; Eph. 3:8-11):**

A. The Lord Jesus was God incarnated in the flesh, and His flesh was a tabernacle in which God could dwell on earth (John 1:14); the Lord's divine element was confined in His humanity, just as God's shekinah glory had been concealed within the tabernacle.

B. Once, on the Mount of Transfiguration, the Lord's divine element was released from within His flesh and expressed in glory, being seen by three disciples, but then it was concealed again in His flesh (Matt. 17:1-4; John 1:14).

C. Before His prayer in John 17, He predicted that He would be glorified and that the Father would be glorified in Him; now He was about to pass through death so that the concealing shell of His humanity might be broken and His divine element, His divine life, might be released (12:23; 13:31-32).

D. Also, He would resurrect so that He might uplift His humanity into the divine element and so that His divine element might be expressed, with the result that His entire being, His divinity and humanity, would be glorified; the Father would thus be glorified in Him; hence, He prayed for this (Luke 12:49-50; John 12:23-24; 17:1).

Day 2
korran

E. The Lord's prayer here concerning the divine mystery of glorification is fulfilled in three stages:

1. First, it was fulfilled in His resurrection, in that His divine element, His divine life, was

released from within His humanity into His many believers (12:23-24), and His whole being, including His humanity, was brought into glory (Luke 24:26; cf. 1 Cor. 15:45b; Acts 13:33; Rom. 1:3-4; Col. 1:18; 1 Pet. 1:3), and in that the Father's divine element was expressed in His resurrection and glorification; in His resurrection God answered and fulfilled His prayer (Acts 3:13-15).

2. Second, it has been fulfilled in the church, in that as His resurrection life has been expressed through His many members, He has been glorified in them, and the Father has been glorified in Him through the church (Eph. 3:21; 1 Tim. 3:15-16).

3. Third, it will ultimately be fulfilled in the New Jerusalem, in that He will be fully expressed in glory, and God will be glorified in Him through the holy city for eternity (Rev. 21:11, 23-24).

Day 3

Harolds

F. In the Lord's last words to the believers in John 14 through 16, there are three concrete expressions of this glory: the Father's house (the church) in 14:2, the branches of the vine (the constituents of the Body of Christ) in 15:1-5, and a newborn corporate man (the new man) in 16:21:

1. All three denote the church, showing that the church is the glorious increase produced by Christ through His death and resurrection (12:23-24).

2. In this glorious increase Christ, the Son of God, is glorified, causing God the Father also to be glorified in Christ's glorification, that is, to be fully expressed through the church (17:1, 4; Eph. 3:19-21; cf. 1 Cor. 6:20; 10:31).

3. This expression needs to be maintained in the oneness of the Triune God; therefore, the Lord prayed in particular for this matter in His concluding prayer in John 17.

    4. The top attribute of the Triune God is oneness; thus, for Him to be glorified, expressed, in His believers is for Him to be expressed in His oneness (v. 21).

II. **The Lord's prayer in John 17 was for the oneness of the Body of Christ, the oneness of the believers in the Triune God:**

Day 4

A. The first level of oneness is the oneness in the Father's name and by the Father's divine life (vv. 6-13):

    1. The Father's name denotes the person of the Father, the Father Himself as the source of life, the source of oneness (vv. 6, 11; 5:26, 43):

      a. We must take the Father as the source of life and blessing (cf. Matt. 14:19; Rom. 11:36).

      b. We must not live by our human life but by the Father's divine life in our spirit to enjoy our all-inclusive sonship (John 6:57; Rom. 8:15-16).

    2. The Father's life with His nature is the element of the oneness (John 17:2; cf. Eph. 1:4-5; Heb. 2:10-11; 1 Cor. 6:17).

Day 5

B. The second level of oneness is the oneness in the reality of the sanctifying word (John 17:14-21):

    1. The Father's word is the truth (v. 17), and the truth is the Triune God (14:6; 1 John 5:6b); to be sanctified by the reality of the word is to be sanctified by the Triune God Himself.

    2. The word, which is the truth, sanctifies God's people from the world (John 17:17) and keeps them from the ruler of the world, the evil one (v. 15):

      a. The Father's word of reality sanctifies us and makes us pure, delivering us from the mixed-up world to separate us unto our God, the God of purity; the more a person is in the word of God, the purer he becomes (Psa. 12:6; 119:140).

      b. The Father's sanctifying word is the means

of our oneness, bringing us into the sphere of oneness (John 17:21; Eph. 5:26).

C. The third level of oneness is the oneness in the divine glory for the expression of the processed, mingled, and incorporated Triune God (John 17:22-24):

1. The oneness of all the believers in the divine glory is the oneness in the expressed sonship with the Father's life and nature (v. 22; 5:26).

2. The glory of God is the expression of God; this splendid expression of divinity delivers us from our self and makes us fully one (cf. Rev. 21:11).

3. In this stage of the oneness the self is fully denied:

   a. We must be saved from our self, including ambition, self-exaltation, and opinions and concepts (John 17:21-23; Rom. 5:10; 1 Cor. 1:10-13; 3 John 9).

   b. If we would give up the self, lose the self, and turn to the spirit, right away we would be in the reality of the Body (Eph. 2:22; John 16:13).

   c. If we live by our life with our nature to express ourselves, there will be no glory of God; in the expression of ourselves there is division.

   d. To live and act in the Father's life with the Father's nature to express the Father is glory, and it is in this glory that we all are one.

4. Our Christian life should be a life of "glory to glory" (2 Cor. 3:16-18).

III. **We need to emphasize the oneness that the Lord has given us and that to preserve this oneness we need to be constantly mingled with the Triune God (thus nullifying the natural man, the world with Satan, and the self) to satisfy the Lord's desire (Eph. 4:1-6).**

Day 6

Morning Nourishment

John These things Jesus spoke, and lifting up His eyes to
17:1 heaven, He said, Father, the hour has come; glorify
      Your Son that the Son may glorify You.
 4-5 I have glorified You on earth, finishing the work
      which You have given Me to do. And now, glorify
      Me along with Yourself, Father, with the glory
      which I had with You before the world was.

The basic concept of the Lord's prayer in John 17 is glorification....This is the subject, the central point, of this prayer. If we see
the main points of the three previous chapters, we shall be able to
understand what it means to have the Son glorified that the Father
may be glorified. The Father is to glorify the Son so that the
Son may glorify the Father. This is a mutual glorification between
the Son and the Father. If the Father will glorify the Son, then the
Son will glorify the Father. (*Life-study of John*, pp. 456-457)

Today's Reading

As a prayer that follows a message conveys the main point
of the message, so the Lord's concluding prayer [in John 17] covers the main point of the message He gave in the preceding three
chapters....In what way is the Father to be glorified in the
Son?...The organism of the vine tree is for the propagating and
spreading of life, that is, for the multiplication and reproduction of
life, and also for the expression of the Triune God. When the Triune God is propagated, multiplied, and expressed through this
organism, the Son is glorified, and in the Son's glorification the
Father is glorified also. Thus, the Lord prayed that He, the Son,
would be glorified so that the Father also might be glorified.

God's eternal purpose, His ultimate intention, is to manifest, to
express, Himself....Glorification simply means manifestation.
To be glorified is to be manifested and expressed.

God's intention in creating man in His own image was that He
might be expressed. The Lord Jesus is God who became incarnated
as a man for the purpose of declaring the invisible God. John 1:18
says that no one has ever seen God but that the Son has declared

Him. God is unseen and invisible. No one except the Son of God has ever seen Him. Now, in His incarnation, the Son has declared Him. To declare God means to express God. The Lord Jesus is the very image of the invisible God (Col. 1:15), which means that He is the very expression of the invisible God.

The blossoming [of a flower] is the glorification of the seed, for it is by blossoming that the seed is glorified, that is, expressed. When Jesus Christ came in the flesh, He was like…[a] little carnation seed. In Him, that is, in His human form, His human shell, were all the beauty and shape of the divine life.…One day, He was sown into the earth. After He died, He grew up and blossomed in His resurrection. In His resurrection, the beauty, form, style, color, and riches of life were released and expressed. That was the glorification of the Son. Since all that God the Father is has been embodied in the Son, when the Son is glorified, the Father is also glorified in the Son's glorification.

After the Lord became flesh, He expressed God to some extent, but the glory of God, the glory of all His attributes, was hidden in His flesh. The glory of all God's fullness was covered, being clothed by His flesh.…His flesh was a tabernacle for God's dwelling on earth (John 1:14). His divine element was confined in His humanity, just as God's shekinah glory was concealed within the tabernacle. Once, on the Mount of Transfiguration, His divine element was released from within His flesh and expressed in glory, being seen by three of the disciples (Matt. 17:1-4; John 1:14). But it was concealed again in His flesh.…He had to pass through death that the concealing shell of His humanity might be broken for His divine element, His divine life, to be released. He also had to be resurrected that He might uplift His humanity into the divine element and that His divine element might be expressed so that His entire being, both divinity and humanity, might be glorified. In this way, the Father would be glorified in Him. In John 17 He prayed for this. (*Life-study of John*, pp. 457-459)

Further Reading: Life-study of John, msg. 38

Enlightenment and inspiration: _____

_____

_____

_____

Morning Nourishment

John   ...The hour has come for the Son of Man to be glori-
12:23-24 fied. Truly, truly, I say to you, Unless the grain of
          wheat falls into the ground and dies, it abides alone;
          but if it dies, it bears much fruit.
Luke   Was it not necessary for the Christ to suffer these
24:26   things and enter into His glory?
Eph.   To Him be the glory in the church and in Christ Jesus
3:21   unto all the generations forever and ever. Amen.

The fulfillment, the answer, of this prayer for the glorification of the Triune God [in John 17] has three stages. The first stage was the Lord's resurrection. In the Lord's resurrection, all the life beauty, life essence, life color, life shape, and all the aspects of the divine life of the Triune God were released. In His resurrection, the Lord's divine life was released from within His humanity and imparted into His many believers (12:23-24), and His whole being, including His humanity, was brought into glory (Luke 24:26), and, in that, the Father's divine element was expressed. God firstly answered and fulfilled this prayer in the Lord's resurrection (Acts 3:13-15). (*Life-study of John*, pp. 459-460)

Today's Reading

Secondly, this prayer [in John 17] has been fulfilled in the church, in that, as His resurrection life has been expressed through His many members, He has been glorified in them and the Father has also been glorified in Him through the church (Eph. 3:21; 1 Tim. 3:15-16). Look at the church in Acts on the day of Pentecost. There we see the beauty, shape, and riches of the divine life....From the day of resurrection until the second coming of the Lord is the age of the church. In this age, the Lord has been glorifying Himself in the believers. Throughout all generations, the Son of God has been and still is being glorified....If we say that we are coming together to exhibit Christ, it means that we are glorifying Christ and making Him manifested. If we say that we are testifying for the Lord, it means that we are manifesting Christ through us. The testimony of the Lord is the manifestation and glorification of the Lord through us. If we want a testimony for the Lord Jesus on our jobs, in school, and in many other places, it means that we want the Lord Jesus to be manifested through us....When the Lord is manifested and glorified through us, the Father is also glorified in the Lord at the same time. Thus, the Lord's prayer is still being fulfilled today through the church.

What is the third stage of the fulfillment of the Lord's prayer in John 17? It is the New Jerusalem....Through the holy city the Son will be fully expressed in glory, and God will also be glorified in Him for eternity (Rev. 21:11, 23-24). Look at the picture of the New Jerusalem: it is a vessel to express Christ, to make God expressed through Christ. The New Jerusalem is the glorification of the Son so that the Father might be glorified through the Son.

The first stage of the fulfillment was the resurrection of Jesus. By His resurrection, the Lord Jesus has been manifested and glorified, and by this glorification the Father has also been glorified. The second step of its fulfillment is in the church. From the day of Pentecost to the day of the Lord's second coming, the Holy Spirit has manifested and will continue to manifest Christ through the saints. In other words, the Holy Spirit glorifies Christ through the church. When Christ is glorified, the Father also is glorified in the Son. The last stage of the fulfillment of this prayer will occur when the fullness of time comes. At that time, all the redeemed ones of both the Old and New Testament will be composed together as the complete expression of the Triune God. In this complete expression, Christ will be the lamp and God will be the light. Christ will be manifested and glorified through the New Jerusalem, and God the Father will be manifested and glorified in the Son as well as through the New Jerusalem. That will be the complete fulfillment of the Lord's word, "Glorify Your Son that the Son may glorify You" [John 17:1]. (*Life-study of John*, pp. 460, 462-463)

Further Reading: The Oneness and the One Accord according to the Lord's Aspiration and the Body Life and Service according to His Pleasure, ch. 2

Enlightenment and inspiration: _____

_____

_____

_____

Morning Nourishment

John In My Father's house are many abodes;...for I go to
14:2 prepare a place for you.
15:5 I am the vine; you are the branches. He who abides
      in Me and I in him, he bears much fruit; for apart
      from Me you can do nothing.
16:21 A woman, when she gives birth, has sorrow because
      her hour has come; but when she brings forth the little
      child, she no longer remembers the affliction because
      of the joy that a man has been born into the world.

In the Lord's last words to the believers in John 14—16, there are three concrete, corporate expressions of...glory: the Father's house (the church) in 14:2, the branches of the vine (the constituents of the Body of Christ) in 15:1-5, and a newborn corporate man (the new man) in 16:21. All three denote the church, showing that the church is the glorious increase produced by the glorious Christ through His death and resurrection. In this glorious increase, Christ, the Son of God, is glorified, causing God the Father also to be glorified in Christ's glorification, that is, to be fully expressed through the church (Eph. 3:19-21). This expression needs to be maintained in the oneness of the Triune God. Therefore, the Lord prayed in particular for this matter in His concluding prayer in John 17 (vv. 20-23). This glorious increase of Christ is the peak of the mystery revealed in the Gospel of John, and its ultimate consummation is the New Jerusalem in Revelation.... The new holy city will be the aggregate of Christ's increase throughout the generations, and in it Christ's divine glory will be expressed to the uttermost. In the glorifying of God the Son, God the Father also will obtain eternal, matchless glory, which will be His full expression in eternity. Thus His eternal economy will be fulfilled for eternity. (John 12:24, footnote 2)

Today's Reading

This oneness was something in the Lord's desire. This desire of the Lord's became His aspiration, and this aspiration was expressed in the prayer offered by the Lord in John 17 (vv. 2, 6, 11, 14-24). The subject of the Lord's prayer in John 17 is oneness. The Lord uttered this prayer out of the divine aspiration. At that time this oneness was not yet a reality; however, a model of this oneness—the oneness among the Three of the Divine Trinity—was there. The Father and the Son are one (vv. 11, 21), and this oneness implies or includes the Spirit. In John 17 the Lord used the plural pronouns *We* (v. 11) and *Us* (v. 21) to signify the Triune God. The Triune God is one, and that oneness is a model of the oneness of the Body of Christ. Because the oneness of the Body has the oneness among the Three of the Trinity as a model, John 17 tells us that this oneness is altogether wrapped up with the Triune God (v. 21). The oneness of the Body of Christ is just the enlarged oneness of the Divine Trinity. The model was there at the time the Lord prayed, but the enlargement was still to come. This enlarged oneness came on the day of Pentecost. Through the outpouring of the Spirit, the Body of Christ was produced (1 Cor. 12:13). That Body is the solid oneness. (*The Intrinsic Problem in the Lord's Recovery Today and Its Scriptural Remedy*, pp. 10-11)

The most difficult thing among Christians is to keep the oneness....There is no other way [to reproduce the divine oneness as the copy of the oneness among the Three of the Godhead] except by enjoying the Triune God. We need to enjoy Him to the extent that the Three of the divine Godhead can be expressed. Then the oneness is among us. This reproduced oneness is the issue of our enjoyment of the Triune God....In order to keep the oneness, we need to reject, renounce, and deny anything that we have that is outside of the Triune God....Anything other than the Triune God Himself can become a dividing factor. We are perfected into one by having the Divine Trinity in us. (*Living in and with the Divine Trinity*, pp. 133-134)

Further Reading: The Intrinsic Problem in the Lord's Recovery Today and Its Scriptural Remedy, ch. 1

Enlightenment and inspiration: _____

_____

_____

_____

Morning Nourishment

John I have manifested Your name to the men whom You
17:6 gave Me out of the world....
  11 ...Holy Father, keep them in Your name, which You
        have given to Me, that they may be one even as We are.
6:57 As the living Father has sent Me and I live because
        of the Father, so he who eats Me, he also shall live
        because of Me.

Your name, [in John 17:6] and in verse 26, means the very name *Father....*The Son came and worked in the Father's name (5:43; 10:25) to manifest the Father to the men whom the Father gave Him and to make the Father's name known to them (v. 26). That name reveals the Father as the source of life (5:26) for the propagation and multiplication of life. Many sons would be born of the Father (1:12-13) to express the Father. Hence, the Father's name is very much related to the divine life. (John 17:6, footnote 1)

The Son's believers are still in the world. They need to be kept that they may be one even as the Divine Trinity is one, that is, that they may be one in the Divine Trinity. The Son prayed that the holy Father would so keep them. (John 17:11, footnote 1)

To be kept in the Father's name is to be kept by His life, because only those who are born of the Father and have the Father's life can participate in the Father's name. The Son has given the Father's life to those whom the Father has given Him (v. 2); hence, they share the Father's name by being kept in it, and they are one in it. The first aspect of this oneness, that is, the first aspect of the building up of the believers, is the oneness in the Father's name and by His divine life. In this aspect of oneness the believers, born of the Father's life, enjoy the Father's name, that is, the Father Himself, as the factor of their oneness. (John 17:11, footnote 2)

Today's Reading

We need to properly consider...three levels of oneness. The first level of oneness is the oneness of all the believers in the Father's name and life. What is the meaning of the Father's name? The

Father's name denotes the person of the Father, who is the Father Himself. The Father is the source of life. The oneness of the believers originates from the Father Himself (the person), who is the source of life. Since the first level of the oneness which the Lord desires originates from the Father as the source, there is no need for our own person. We are not the source. Only the Father is the source. Hence, we should not live by our human life. We should live by the Father's divine life. Only the Father's life is the source. Hence, basically speaking, we have to see that the oneness of the believers for which the Lord Jesus prays is with the Father as the source rather than with man as the source.

Furthermore, this oneness is in the Father's life. The Father denotes the source, and the Father's life denotes the element. The Father's life is the element for oneness. Hence, the oneness that we pursue after is the oneness of life, which is of the Father as the source. This oneness has the Father as the source and His life as the element. This sounds simple, but its requirements are stringent. Everything of what we are and do must be terminated. In this way, regardless how many thousands and millions of saints there are, if there is only one source with only one inward essence, there will surely be oneness. Hence, this oneness is not according to what most Christians would consider. It is not a oneness of people clustering together and convinced by one another to have the same thought and opinion. This is a muddy oneness. It is not a golden oneness. The oneness the Lord wants is one in which we have the same source and the same life, taking the Father as the source and living by His life. When the Father's life with His nature becomes the element of oneness in us, we will spontaneously be one. (*The Oneness and the One Accord according to the Lord's Aspiration and the Body Life and Service according to His Pleasure*, pp. 12-13)

Further Reading: The Oneness and the One Accord according to the Lord's Aspiration and the Body Life and Service according to His Pleasure, ch. 1; *Life-study of John*, msg. 39

Enlightenment and inspiration: _____

_____

_____

_____

Morning Nourishment

John
17:17-21
Sanctify them in the truth; Your word is truth. As You have sent Me into the world, I also have sent them into the world. And for their sake I sanctify Myself, that they themselves also may be sanctified in truth. And I do not ask concerning these only, but concerning those also who believe into Me through their word, that they all may be one; even as You, Father, are in Me and I in You, that they also may be in Us; that the world may believe that You have sent Me.

The second aspect of the believers' oneness [is] the oneness in the Triune God through sanctification, separation from the world by the word of God. In this aspect of oneness the believers, separated from the world unto God, enjoy the Triune God as the factor of their oneness. (John 17:21, footnote 1)

The second level of oneness is the oneness of all the believers in the reality of the Father's sanctifying word. The Lord has given us the Father's name and His eternal life. But He did not ask us to leave the world. How then should we live in the world? For this purpose, He has given us the Father's word. The Father's word has God Himself as the reality. God as the reality is in His word. Without God's word, we cannot touch God's reality. Today God is in His word. This word contains the reality of God, which is God Himself. God Himself as this reality has a special function, which is to sanctify us. Those of us who read God's word frequently have this experience. Whether or not we understand the Bible, as long as we read a little of God's Word in the morning and consider this Word a little during the day, we are sanctified. (*The Oneness and the One Accord according to the Lord's Aspiration and the Body Life and Service according to His Pleasure*, pp. 13-14)

Today's Reading

One saint confessed that his mind was not sharp and that he tended to forget about the things he read in the Bible. Brother

Watchman Nee comforted him by saying that it was all right to forget what one had read in the Bible. He illustrated by saying that when one takes a bamboo basket to the river to wash the rice in the basket, one drops the basket in and out of the water many times. Although no water is left in the basket, the basket itself and the rice in it are all washed clean. Many times we exert great effort in memorizing the words of the Bible, only to find that after a few days we remember nothing; everything seems to be gone. But in fact, when we read the Lord's Word again and again, all the worldly matters in us are removed, and we are cleansed and sanctified. God's word brings in God's reality, and in us it produces a special effect, which is to sanctify us and to deliver us from this mixed world that we may be separated unto God.

The world is very mixed. But God's word of reality sanctifies us and makes us pure. The result of this purity is holiness. Anything that is separated is pure. The more a person is in the word of God, the purer he becomes. A man who is not in God's word but is in the world is complicated and impure. He may not be very literate, yet he can still be very complicated within. However, if we have God's word within, this word with God's reality will do a sanctifying work within us to separate us unto God, thus making us pure. God is on the side of purity, and Satan as the prince of the world is on the side of complication. Satan is the prince of the mixed-up world, but our God is the God of purity. The word of reality sanctifies us and delivers us from the mixed-up world, turning us back to the purity in God. In this way, we are one.

Hence, the Father's name is the source of our oneness; the Father's life is the element of our oneness; and the Father's sanctifying word is the means of our oneness, bringing us to the sphere of oneness. Because of the Father, not only is our source one and our nature one, but where we are also becomes one. (*The Oneness and the One Accord according to the Lord's Aspiration and the Body Life and Service according to His Pleasure,* p. 14)

Further Reading: Life-study of John, msg. 40

Enlightenment and inspiration: _____

_____

_____

_____

Morning Nourishment

John And the glory which You have given Me I have given
17:22-23   to them, that they may be one, even as We are one; I in
them, and You in Me, that they may be perfected into
one, that the world may know that You have sent Me
and have loved them even as You have loved Me.

The glory that the Father gave to the Son is the sonship with
the Father's life and divine nature (John 5:26). The sonship was
given so that the Son could express the Father in His fullness
(1:18; 14:9; Col. 2:9; Heb. 1:3). The Son has given this glory to His
believers that they too may have the sonship with the Father's life
and divine nature (John 17:2; 2 Pet. 1:4) to express the Father in
the Son in the Son's fullness (John 1:16). (John 17:22, footnote 1)

The third aspect of the believers' oneness [is] the oneness in
the divine glory for the corporate expression of God. In this aspect
of oneness the believers, their self having been fully denied, enjoy
the glory of the Father as the factor of their perfected oneness and
thus express God in a corporate, built-up way. This is the oneness
of the divine commission; it fulfills the Son's prayer that He be
fully expressed, that is, glorified, in the building up of the believers, and that the Father be fully expressed, glorified, in the Son's
glorification. Hence, the ultimate oneness of the believers is (1) in
the eternal life of God (in the Father's name), (2) by the holy word
of God, and (3) in the divine glory to express the Triune God for
eternity. That the Son might accomplish this oneness, the Father
gave Him six things: the authority (17:2), the believers (vv. 2, 6, 9,
24), the work (v. 4), the words (v. 8), the Father's name (vv. 11-12),
and the Father's glory (v. 24). That the believers may participate
in this oneness, the Son gave them three things: the eternal life
(v. 2), the holy word of God (vv. 8, 14), and the divine glory (v. 22).
(So also for *one* in v. 23.) (John 17:22, footnote 2)

Today's Reading

The third level of the oneness is the oneness of all the believers
in the expression of the divine glory. In John 17:22 the Lord Jesus

said to the Father, "And the glory which You have given Me I have given to them, that they may be one, even as We are one." According to the revelation of the Bible and in comparison with our experience, glory here refers to the Father's life with His nature to express His divine virtue. Hence, the glory of God is the expression of God. Glory is not a sudden kind of beam that shines on us and surrounds us from without. Rather, it is the Father's divine life with the divine nature, expressing a kind of divine radiance and splendor. This divine, splendid expression delivers us from ourselves and makes us fully one.

The first level of the oneness is in the Father's name and life, delivering us from the natural realm. The second level of the oneness is in the reality of the Father's sanctifying word, delivering us from the world. Now the third level of the oneness is in the Father's glory, delivering us from ourselves and causing us to become fully one in the Triune God. We have to realize that this oneness is the Body of Christ; it is the real and practical church. The church is the oneness lived out of the believers in the Triune God. This oneness has God as the source and His life as the essence, in which the radiance and splendor in divinity are fully expressed through God's life and nature in a sanctified realm. This is the practical church life. This is also the building. It is something we ought to treasure and pursue.

We should all be clear that the oneness of the Lord's believers is not as we imagined. It is not a oneness arrived at by dropping our opinions and agreeing mutually with one another. The genuine oneness of the church is a oneness in which we have the Father Himself as the source, the Father's life as the nature, and the Father's sanctifying reality as the realm, which enables us to live in purity, being unrelated to the world, and which expresses the divine radiance and splendor through God's life with His nature. This oneness is the Body of Christ; it is also the building God is after. (*The Oneness and the One Accord according to the Lord's Aspiration and the Body Life and Service according to His Pleasure*, p. 15)

Further Reading: Life-study of John, msg. 41

Enlightenment and inspiration: _____

_____

_____

_____

Hymns, #1081   , 1240, 1226

1   Father God, Thou art the source of life.
    We, Thy sons, are Thine expression;
    In Thy name, our dear possession.
    Father God, Thou art the source of life.

       In Thy life, in Thy life,
       We have oneness in Thy life.
       In Thy life, in Thy life,
       In Thy life, O Father, we are one.

2   How we thank Thee that Thy holy Word
    With Thy nature, saturates us;
    From the world it separates us.
    Thank Thee, Father, for Thy holy Word.

       Through Thy Word, through Thy Word,
       We have oneness through Thy Word.
       Through Thy Word, through Thy Word,
       Through Thy holy Word we're all made one.

3   Oh, the glory of the Triune God!
    We're His sons, oh, what a blessing!
    We His glory are expressing—
    Oh, the glory of the Triune God!

       In Thy glory, in Thy glory,
       In Thy glory we are one.
       In Thy glory, in Thy glory,
       In Thy glory we are all made one!

Composition for prophecy with main point and sub-points: _____

_____

_____

_____

_____

_____

_____

_____

_____

_____

_____

_____

_____

_____

_____

_____

_____

_____

_____

_____

_____

_____

_____

_____

_____

_____

_____

_____

_____

_____

_____

_____

_____

_____

_____

_____

_____

The Oneness of the Body of Christ— the Oneness in the Triune God Typified by the Tabernacle

Scripture Reading: Exo. 26:15, 24, 26-29; John 17:21-23; Eph. 4:2-3

Day 1

Martins

4X12

I. The oneness for which the Lord prayed in John 17 is the oneness typified by the tabernacle in Exodus 26; because the forty-eight boards of the tabernacle typify the believers built together to be the dwelling place of God, the tabernacle is a clear picture of the oneness in the Triune God.

II. The first aspect of the oneness in the Triune God is seen with the three gold rings (the receptacles for the uniting bars), which signify the initial Spirit, the regenerating and sealing Spirit, the all-inclusive Spirit of the Triune God in resurrection for the uniting of the believers (vv. 15, 24, 29; John 3:6; Eph. 1:13; 4:3, 30; cf. Gen. 24:22; Luke 15:22).

Day 2

(6P)

Warrens

III. The second aspect of the oneness in the Triune God is seen in the overlaying of the boards (signifying the believers with the human nature) with gold (signifying God with the divine nature) (Exo. 26:29):

A. The oneness of the boards of the tabernacle was not in the acacia wood but in the gold that overlaid the wood; this portrays that the oneness in the church is not in our humanity but in the Triune God with His divine nature (John 17:21).

B. The oneness of the boards was not only in the gold, signifying God, but also in the shining of the gold, the expression of the gold, signifying the glory of God; our oneness today is in the Triune God and in His glory, His shining, His expression (vv. 22-24).

C. The initial Spirit, who is the Triune God typified by the gold, is the oneness of the Spirit (Eph. 4:3);

the overlaying of the gold is actually the spreading of the oneness:

1. The more we are overlaid with gold, the more
   oneness we have; the more we have of God,
   the stronger our oneness is (cf. Col. 2:19).

Day 3
2. Instead of being overlaid with gold, we may
   be merely gilded with gold, like Babylon the
   Great in Revelation 17:4; the amount of gold
   that we have may not be enough to keep us in
   the genuine oneness.

3. Only when the boards were adequately overlaid with gold were they perfected into one;
   this indicates that to be perfected into one is
   to gain more of God (John 17:23).

D. "Not having an adequate amount of God can create
   a serious problem with the oneness. The Lord's
   recovery is not a movement. We do not desire to
   gain a large number of people. In the recovery we
   are concerned for the genuine weight of gold. The
   important question is this: How much of God do
   you have? The Lord's recovery consists of God overlaying His recovered people with Himself" (*Truth
   Messages*, p. 86).

E. Oneness is a matter of sinking deeply into the Triune God until we are fully overlaid with gold; our
   problem is that we are short of God, and our need
   is to gain more of Him (Col. 2:19; Phil. 3:8b):

1. Everything depends upon how much gold we
   have; we all can become dissenting if we are
   short of gold.

2. Today the Lord needs this genuine oneness; if
   we do not have this oneness, we cannot go on
   in the recovery.

3. The only way to be kept in this solid, real oneness is to have an adequate amount of the
   experienced God (v. 10).

Day 4
F. The golden nature of God will never overlay our
   fallen nature but will overlay only our regenerated
   and transformed nature, signified by acacia wood:

  1. The overlaying of gold occurs simultaneously with this transformation; wherever transformation is, there the overlaying of the gold is also.

  2. Transformation depends upon our loving the Lord, our contacting Him, our listening to His word, our praying to Him, and our walking according to the spirit; as long as we have these five things, we are living Christ (Rom. 8:4; Phil. 1:19-21a).

  3. Only when we all have been transformed and overlaid with gold will it no longer be possible for there to be dissension among us; the only safeguard is to be overlaid with gold (2 Cor. 3:18; Rom. 12:2).

Day 5

IV. **The third aspect of the oneness in the Triune God is seen with the uniting bars, which held the forty-eight boards together and brought them into oneness; these uniting bars signify the initial Spirit becoming the uniting Spirit to join all the members of Christ into one Body (Exo. 26:26-29; Eph. 4:3):**

  A. The uniting bars were made of acacia wood for connecting strength and overlaid with gold for uniting; that the bars were made of acacia wood indicates that the oneness of the Spirit involves not only Christ's divinity but also His humanity (cf. v. 2, footnote 1).

  B. In actuality, the uniting bars signify not the Holy Spirit alone but the Holy Spirit mingled with our human spirit (Rom. 8:16)—the mingled spirit, which includes both divinity and humanity.

  C. The uniting of the boards of the tabernacle involved the passing of the bars through the rings on each board to join the boards together; this signifies that the believers in Christ are united when their spirit cooperates with the Spirit, thus allowing the uniting Spirit to pass through them to join them to other believers.

Day 6

  D. In order for the uniting Spirit to pass through us

and thus join us with others, we need to receive the cross, for the uniting Spirit always crosses the standing boards (Matt. 16:24):

1. The Spirit brings us to the cross, the cross is applied by the Spirit, and the cross issues in more of the Spirit (Exo. 30:22-25; Phil. 1:19):
   a. The Spirit of the crucified Christ is always bringing us to the cross, conforming us to the death of Christ, and the cross is applied by the Spirit (1 Cor. 1:23; 2:2; Gal. 5:22-24; Phil. 3:10; Rom. 8:13).
   b. The experience of the cross of Christ issues in the abundance of the Spirit of life (Gal. 2:20; John 12:24).
2. We are joined into one by our spirit (with our mind, will, and emotion) cooperating with the crossing Spirit; whenever our spirit is one with the crossing Spirit, we experience the uniting Spirit.
3. The initial Spirit must become the uniting Spirit within us; then we will have the oneness and the building, and we will be safeguarded from dissension and division.

Morning Nourishment

John   That they all may be one; even as You, Father, are
17:21   in Me and I in You, that they also may be in Us...
Exo.   And you shall overlay the boards with gold, and
26:29-30 make their rings of gold as holders for the bars;
        and you shall overlay the bars with gold. And you
        shall set up the tabernacle according to its plan,
        which you were shown in the mountain.

In John 17 the Lord Jesus prayed that we would be one in the
Triune God. This concept is deep and profound, far beyond our understanding. In verse 23 the Lord said, "I in them, and You in Me,
that they may be perfected into one." Such a word surpasses our
comprehension. However, if we consider the type of the tabernacle
in Exodus 26, we shall find it much easier to grasp the meaning of
the Lord's prayer for oneness in John 17.

The building of the tabernacle in Exodus corresponds to the
oneness in John 17. The Lord prayed that all His believers would
be one so that God could have a dwelling place on earth. The tabernacle was such a dwelling place. The oneness seen in the tabernacle
is simply the building of the tabernacle. The tabernacle had forty-
eight boards. Because these boards were built together to be the
dwelling place of God, the tabernacle is a clear picture of the oneness in the Triune God. This oneness is not in the acacia wood out
of which the boards were made; it is in the gold that overlaid them.
The wood and the gold signify the Christian's human and divine
nature. The human nature is signified by the acacia wood, and the
divine nature, by the gold. Each board was made of acacia wood
overlaid with gold. Because we Christians are both wooden and
golden, we are wonderful. (*Truth Messages,* pp. 81, 101)

Today's Reading

This oneness has three aspects. The first aspect, the initial
aspect, is with the golden rings. I am quite certain that the golden
rings were attached to the boards before the boards were overlaid
with gold. Thus, the first step was to attach the rings to the boards
and the second step was to overlay the boards with gold. The third

step was to make the uniting bars, which held the forty-eight
boards together and brought them into oneness. This oneness is
the building, which is the dwelling place of God.

Since my youth I have devoted much attention to John 17. But
because I was short of experience and did not see the picture of
the oneness portrayed in the tabernacle, I did not have an adequate understanding of the Lord's prayer for oneness in John 17.
But now, after years of experience and even of suffering, I can say
that the oneness for which the Lord prayed in John 17 is the very
oneness seen in the tabernacle. By considering the picture of the
tabernacle, we can have the proper understanding of the practical
oneness for which the Lord Jesus prayed.

This oneness is in the Triune God. The boards were one in the
gold, and the gold signifies the nature of God....On each board
there were the three rings signifying the Triune God, who is the
sealing Spirit we have received. This Spirit is not merely the
Spirit of God, but the Spirit of God with the Father and the Son. In
John the Lord Jesus said that the Spirit would be sent from the
Father (15:26)....The Spirit is sent not only from the Father but
also with the Father [see footnote 1 on v. 26]. After He sent the
Spirit, the Father did not remain in the heavens. No, when the
Father sent the Spirit, the Spirit came to us with the Father.
Therefore, to have the Spirit in us is also to have the Father in us.
In like manner, the Son is with the Father. From eternity to eter-
nity, the Son has always been and always will be with the Father.
Therefore, to have the Spirit in us is also to have the Father and
the Son in us. Hence, we have the Triune God as the three rings.
The Father is embodied in the Son, and the Son is realized as the
Spirit. Therefore, when we have the Spirit, we have the Father
and the Son. This is the initial Spirit, the sealing Spirit, we have
received as the rings. This life-giving Spirit has regenerated us
and now is dwelling in us. (*Truth Messages,* pp. 102-103)

Further Reading: The Intrinsic Problem in the Lord's Recovery
  Today and Its Scriptural Remedy, ch. 1

Enlightenment and inspiration: _____

_____

_____

_____

Morning Nourishment

Exo. **And you shall make the boards for the tabernacle**
26:15 **of acacia wood, standing up.**
  29 **And you shall overlay the boards with gold...**
John **And the glory which You have given Me I have given**
17:22 **to them, that they may be one, even as We are one.**

In Exodus 26 we have a picture of the oneness in the Triune God. The standing boards of the tabernacle make up a corporate structure....There was a total of forty-eight boards. When these boards were put together, they composed God's dwelling place. To be sure, God's dwelling place is a corporate matter. Hence, in the tabernacle with the forty-eight standing boards we see a picture of real oneness. In order to become one entity as God's dwelling place, the forty-eight boards had to be brought into oneness. They were one, not in the acacia wood, but in the gold that overlaid the wood. (*Truth Messages,* p. 81)

Today's Reading

The Ark is a type of Christ with His two natures: the human nature typified by the acacia wood and the divine nature signified by the gold....These materials were also used in making the boards for the building of God's dwelling place. If the gold had been taken away from the standing boards, leaving only the acacia wood, the boards would immediately have fallen down. Even if they had remained upright, standing side by side, they would still not have been one. Rather, they would have been forty-eight separate, individual boards. Their oneness was not in the acacia wood; it was in the gold. This clearly portrays the fact that our oneness is not in humanity, but in divinity, in the Triune God. If the divine nature were taken away from us, we would immediately become detached from one another. Although we might still love one another and even embrace one another, we nevertheless would not be one. The oneness of the standing boards of the tabernacle, or this oneness in the gold, symbolizes our oneness in the Triune God.

The gold was not only the oneness of the standing boards; it was also their glory. By being overlaid with gold, the standing boards bore the glory of the gold, for the shining of the gold was their glory, their expression. Anyone who entered into the tabernacle could see on every hand the shining of the gold. Hence, the oneness of the forty-eight boards was not only in the gold, signifying God, but also in the shining of the gold, signifying the glory of God. In the same principle, our oneness today is in the Triune God and in His glory, His shining.

My burden in this message is to point out that genuine oneness is absolutely not to be found in our humanity. Do not think that if you are humble or meek you can be one with others. No matter whether we are meek or rough, slow or quick, proud or humble, educated or uneducated, we all have a problem with oneness. In ourselves, by ourselves, and with ourselves we simply cannot be one with others. In fact, we are not always one with ourselves. Once again we need to emphasize that the oneness is in the gold, not in the acacia wood. This means that the oneness in the church is not in our humanity; it is altogether in the Triune God. In the past I wondered why the Lord did not mention such virtues as humility, meekness, and kindness in His prayer for oneness. Instead, He spoke mainly about being in the Triune God. The concept of John 17:21 through 23 is that of oneness in the Triune God. This reveals that oneness is not in humanity; it is only in the Triune God.

The overlaying of the gold is actually the spreading of the oneness. We already have the oneness of the Spirit spoken of in Ephesians 4. This oneness of the Spirit is the gold of the three rings. The initial Spirit, who is the Triune God, is the very oneness of the Spirit. Now this oneness must spread until it overlays our whole being. We have seen that God does not overlay anything natural. Whatever is not acacia wood must be transformed, that is, changed in nature and form. No matter how good our natural being may seem to be, we still need to be transformed. (*Truth Messages*, pp. 81-82, 85, 97)

Further Reading: Truth Messages, ch. 10

Enlightenment and inspiration: _____

_____

_____

_____

1.5 × 48 =

Morning Nourishment

Rev. And the woman was...gilded with gold and precious
17:4-5 stone and pearls....And on her forehead there was a
name written, MYSTERY, BABYLON THE GREAT...
John I in them, and You in Me, that they may be perfected
17:23 into one, that the world may know that You have sent
Me and have loved them even as You have loved Me.

1 cubit
~1.5 ft

Each standing board of the tabernacle was ten cubits high and
one and a half cubits wide. This means its dimensions were fifteen feet in length by twenty-seven inches in width. Certainly a
large amount of gold was required to overlay a board of this size. If
the layer of gold were too thin, it would not have been able to bear
the weight of the board. To prepare the wooden boards was not too
difficult; however, to overlay these large boards was quite a difficult task. Although we all are boards, we may be overlaid with a
very thin layer of gold. Yes, we may be in the Triune God, but we
may not be deeply in Him. Instead of being overlaid with gold,
we may merely be gilded with gold, like Babylon the Great in
Revelation 17. If the standing boards had been only gilded with
gold, there would have been no gold for the rings that supported
the weight of the boards. In order for the forty-eight heavy boards
to be held together, they each had to be overlaid with a heavy
layer of gold. (*Truth Messages*, p. 83)

Today's Reading

In no other portion of the Bible is the Triune God revealed in
such a practical way as in John 17. The various pronouns used—
I, Us, You—indicate that the Triune God is related to our oneness.
It is in the Triune God that we are perfected into one. To be perfected means to have more gold. Only when the boards were
adequately overlaid with gold were they perfected into one. This indicates that to be perfected into one means to gain more of God.
Surely mere teachings about oneness can never make us one.

Oneness is not a superficial matter. It is a matter of sinking
deeply into the Triune God until we are fully overlaid with gold. We
all need a great deal more of God. It is not sufficient simply to be

coated with a thin layer of Him. If we truly have light on our need to be overlaid with gold, we shall repent and say, "Lord, I repent that I am only gilded with gold. I have not yet been overlaid. What I have experienced of You is merely gilding. It is good for causing others to praise me, but it is not good for the real oneness, for holding me together with others. When even a small problem arises, my layer of gold is not sufficient, and the oneness is damaged. Lord, for the oneness, overlay me with an adequate amount of gold."

The more we are overlaid with gold, the more oneness we have. Nothing can damage the oneness that comes from our being overlaid with an ample quantity of gold. The more we have of God, the stronger is our oneness.

Not having an adequate amount of God can create a serious problem with the oneness. The Lord's recovery is not a movement. We do not desire to gain a large number of people. In the recovery we are concerned for the genuine weight of gold. The important question is this: How much of God do you have? The Lord's recovery consists of God overlaying His recovered people with Himself.

Whenever I see that any are dissenting, I feel sorry for them. At the same time I realize that such a situation of dissension is a test, an exposure, and a purification. It is a test of what is real, of how much gold we actually have. We all need to gain more gold. It is not sufficient only to have a good heart, to know the truth, and to care for the Lord's recovery. Everything depends upon how much gold we have. We all can become dissenting if we are short of gold. This should be a warning to us all. Again I say that genuine oneness is possible only in the Triune God.

Today the Lord needs the genuine oneness. If we do not have this oneness, we cannot go on in the recovery. Hence, the most vital and crucial matter is the genuine oneness. The only way to be kept in this solid, real oneness is to have an adequate amount of the experienced God. This is our need today. (*Truth Messages,* pp. 85-88)

Further Reading: Truth Messages, ch. 9

Enlightenment and inspiration: _____

_____

_____

_____

Morning Nourishment

Eph. In whom you also, having heard the word of the truth,
1:13 the gospel of your salvation, in Him also believing, you
were sealed with the Holy Spirit of the promise.
4:30 And do not grieve the Holy Spirit of God, in whom
you were sealed unto the day of redemption.

After we are regenerated, the sealing Spirit begins to spread throughout our being. With some of us this spreading may take place very slowly. Nevertheless, it is going on. Many of us can testify that the spreading of the gold has increased since we came into the Lord's recovery....Being overlaid with gold always goes along with transformation, for the gold only overlays acacia wood. The golden nature of God will never overlay our fallen nature, but will overlay only our regenerated and transformed nature. Our fallen nature is corrupt wood, but our regenerated and transformed nature is acacia wood. This is confirmed by our experience and by observing the experience of many other saints.

We have received not only the seal of the Spirit, but also the sealing of the Spirit....This sealing is spreading in our being, overlaying us with gold. From the time we were regenerated, we have had something very precious within us. By reading the Word we have come to see that this precious substance is the divine nature added to us with God the Spirit. Day by day this Spirit with the divine nature is spreading within us. The more we pray, have fellowship with the Lord, read His Word, and tell Him that we love Him and want to be one with Him, the more we sense that something is spreading within us and overlaying us with gold. (*Truth Messages*, pp. 103-104)

Today's Reading

Transformation has nothing to do with self-correction or self-improvement. Transformation depends upon our loving the Lord, our contacting Him, our listening to His word, our praying to Him, and our walking according to the spirit. As long as we have these five things, we are living Christ. We are taking Christ as our life. Therefore, transformation takes place spontaneously. The overlaying of gold occurs simultaneously with this transformation. Wherever transformation is, there the overlaying gold is also.

Gradually, the Lord showed me that certain dear ones [who damaged the oneness] had nothing more than the three rings. With them, there was no spreading of the gold because there was no transformation. The reason there was no transformation was that in the experience of these dissenting ones there was no dealing of the cross....The standing boards are crossed by the uniting bars. This indicates that although we may be standing upright, the uniting Spirit crosses us. Some today hate the cross; they even despise the word *cross*. But without the cross there can be no resurrection....It is in resurrection that our natural life is transformed. This transformation in resurrection brings in the overlaying gold.

Only when we all have been transformed and overlaid with gold will it no longer be possible for there to be dissension among us....The only safeguard is to be overlaid with gold. We must not go on according to the natural being; instead of a natural humanity we must have a transformed humanity with the very humanity of Jesus as its element....Only the humanity of Jesus, which is a humanity in resurrection, is qualified to be overlaid with gold.

I beg you to bring this matter to the Lord in prayer. We need much prayer in order to realize that the steps to the genuine oneness come from our experience of God....In order to have the reality of this word, we need time and much prayer. The realization of oneness is not easy because it is a divine reality. The divine nature must be wrought into our being. The initial Spirit, the Triune God installed in us as the rings, must spread throughout our being. This spreading requires transformation, and transformation demands that we take Christ as our life by loving Him, contacting Him, listening to His word, praying to Him, and walking in the spirit. If this is our experience, we shall be transformed and overlaid with gold. Then the oneness will be completed within us, and we shall be safeguarded from dissension and division. (*Truth Messages,* pp. 97-99)

Further Reading: Truth Messages, ch. 11

Enlightenment and inspiration: _____

_____

_____

_____

Morning Nourishment

Eph. With all lowliness and meekness, with long-suffering,
4:2-3 bearing one another in love, being diligent to keep
       the oneness of the Spirit in the uniting bond of peace.
Exo. And you shall make bars of acacia wood, five....
26:26-28 And the middle bar shall pass through in the center
       of the boards from end to end.

These virtues [in Ephesians 4:2] are not found in our natural humanity but are in the humanity of Jesus. The fact that the virtues are mentioned here, before the oneness of the Spirit in verse 3, indicates that we must have these virtues in order to keep the oneness of the Spirit. This implies that in the uniting Spirit there is the transformed humanity, the humanity transformed by the resurrection life of Christ. (Eph. 4:2, footnote 1)

Christ abolished on the cross all the differences that were due to ordinances. In so doing He made peace for His Body. This peace should bind all believers together and should thus become the uniting bond. The uniting bond of peace is the issue of the working of the cross. When we remain on the cross, we have peace with others. This peace becomes the uniting bond in which we keep the oneness of the Spirit. (Eph. 4:3, footnote 3)

Today's Reading

Although we may have the initial Spirit and some experience of being overlaid with gold, we still need to go on to the uniting Spirit. After the boards, the rings, and the overlaying gold, we still need the bars. Without the bars, the forty-eight boards cannot be one, for it is the bars that hold them together. What do the bars signify? Since we are the boards, the bars cannot represent us. Furthermore, the rings signify the Triune God, and the gold covering the boards signifies the spreading of God. Just as the rings are a symbol of the initial Spirit, the bars are a symbol of the uniting Spirit. The boards stand upright, and the bars unite them by crossing them horizontally.

Each set of bars contains five bars. The number five is composed of four plus one. One denotes the unique God, and four denotes the creatures. Therefore, the number five signifies the Triune God added to His creatures. The uniting bars are the three-in-one God added to His creatures. The uniting Spirit today is simply the Triune God, the three-in-one God, added to His creatures.

For us, the standing boards, to have acacia wood overlaid with gold is quite understandable. But what does it mean to say that the uniting Spirit has humanity, typified by acacia wood, overlaid with divinity, typified by gold? Some Christian teachers have pointed out that the uniting bars signify the uniting Spirit, but no one has explained why in the uniting Spirit there is acacia wood.

Ephesians 4:2 and 3 help us to understand this matter....Although the oneness is the oneness of the Spirit, it is a oneness we must keep. The keeping of the oneness is our responsibility, not the responsibility of the Spirit. Here we have both divinity, the oneness of the Spirit, and humanity, the keeping of the oneness. If we have the oneness of the Spirit without the keeping of the oneness, we shall be short. Therefore, we need to be diligent to keep the oneness....We must keep the oneness of the Spirit by having lowliness, meekness, and long-suffering and by bearing one another in love. Lowliness, meekness, long-suffering, and the bearing love are all human virtues signified by the acacia wood within the uniting bars. Therefore, in order to keep the oneness of the Spirit, we need a humanity with certain virtues.

The uniting bars are not the Holy Spirit alone, but the Holy Spirit with the human spirit....The uniting bars are not only the Triune God added to man to bear responsibility; the Spirit represented by these bars also includes the human spirit. This means that if our spirit does not cooperate with the uniting Spirit, the oneness cannot be realized in a practical way. The uniting Spirit is actually the mingled spirit. In this mingled spirit there is both divinity and humanity, both gold and acacia wood. (*Truth Messages,* pp. 104-106)

Further Reading: Truth Messages, ch. 11

Enlightenment and inspiration: _____
_____
_____
_____

Morning Nourishment

Matt. Then Jesus said to His disciples, If anyone wants
16:24 to come after Me, let him deny himself and take up
his cross and follow Me.
Rom. ...If by the Spirit you put to death the practices of
8:13 the body, you will live.
16 The Spirit Himself witnesses with our spirit that
we are children of God.

Whether or not the uniting Spirit can actually join us into
one depends on whether or not we are willing to cooperate with
this Spirit. If the Spirit does not have a way to pass through
us, there can be no oneness. In order for the uniting Spirit to
pass through us and thus join us with others, we need to receive
the cross, for the uniting Spirit always crosses the standing
boards. If we are willing to receive the cross, our spirit will cooperate with the uniting Spirit. Then the Spirit with our spirit will
join us to another believer in Christ. We are joined into one by
our spirit cooperating with the crossing Spirit. However, most of
the time we are not willing to be crossed by the Spirit.

The uniting Spirit is seeking to cross through us to others. The
question is whether or not we are willing to go along with Him.
Whenever our spirit is one with the crossing Spirit, we experience
the uniting Spirit. Every time we walk according to the Spirit, we
experience the crossing of the Spirit. We stand, but we are crossed
by the Spirit....When our spirit agrees with the crossing Spirit,
we have the uniting bar. This is the unique way to keep the oneness. This understanding of the uniting bars is confirmed by our
experience. (*Truth Messages*, pp. 106-107)

Today's Reading

The Spirit is continually endeavoring to cross us, to pass
through us. In order for this to take place, our spirit, with our mind,
will, and emotion, must go along with Him. Only then do we have
the uniting bars, the five bars in three rows to unite the believers
into one. When we have all these aspects, we have the oneness in
the Triune God revealed in John 17. This means we have the

building in the overlaying and uniting gold.

If we are willing to be crossed, it means that our spirit goes along with the crossing Spirit. The Spirit will never join us to others without this willingness. The uniting Spirit cannot unite me to you unless your spirit is willing to cooperate with the Spirit.... The uniting Spirit cannot unite us Himself. He must have the cooperation of our spirit. This means that we must be willing to be crossed by Him. (*Truth Messages,* p. 107)

The Spirit brings us to the cross. If we take the cross, the cross will issue in more of the Spirit. Before Christ went to the cross, the Spirit was always leading Him. This leading Spirit always led Him to the cross. The entire life of Christ was a life led by the Spirit to the cross....When we were saved, the first thing we received was the Spirit. Then from that time onward, this Spirit leads us to the cross. We have to undergo the process of being crossed out all the time by allowing the Spirit to bring us to the cross, so that the cross can issue in more of the Spirit.

The Spirit of the crucified Christ is always bringing us to the cross of Christ (1 Cor. 1:23; 2:2; Gal. 5:22-24). As Christians, our destiny is to be crucified, to be crossed out....The Spirit of Christ always leads us to live a crucified life, conforming us to the death of Christ. In Philippians 3:10 Paul said that he desired to know Christ, the power of His resurrection, and the fellowship of His sufferings, being conformed to His death. The wonderful Spirit works to conform us to the death of Christ.

The experience of the cross of Christ issues in the abundance of the Spirit of life. According to Galatians 2:20, the more we experience the cross of Christ, the more Christ lives in us. John 12:24 shows that the Lord's death as a grain of wheat issued in much fruit. When we experience the death of Christ, the issue is the multiplication of life. Furthermore, we boast in the cross of Christ (Gal. 6:14a). The cross was really an abasement, but the apostle Paul made it his boast. (*The Spirit,* pp. 121, 120, 121)

Further Reading: The Spirit, ch. 12

Enlightenment and inspiration: _____

_____

_____

_____

Hymns, #591

1   Not I, but Christ be honored, loved, exalted,
     Not I, but Christ be seen, be known and heard;
     Not I, but Christ in every look and action,
     Not I, but Christ in every thought and word.

     Oh, to be saved from myself, dear Lord,
       Oh, to be lost in Thee,
     Oh, that it may be no more I,
       But Christ that lives in me.

2   Not I, but Christ to gently soothe in sorrow,
     Not I, but Christ to wipe the falling tear;
     Not I, but Christ to lift the weary burden,
     Not I, but Christ to hush away all fear.

3   Christ, only Christ, no idle word e'er falling,
     Christ, only Christ, no needless bustling sound;
     Christ, only Christ, no self-important bearing,
     Christ, only Christ, no trace of I be found.

4   Not I, but Christ my every need supplying,
     Not I, but Christ my strength and health to be;
     Christ, only Christ, for spirit, soul, and body,
     Christ, only Christ, live then Thy life in me.

5   Christ, only Christ, ere long will fill my vision,
     Glory excelling soon, full soon I'll see;
     Christ, only Christ, my every wish fulfilling,
     Christ, only Christ, my all in all to be.

*Composition for prophecy with main point and
sub-points:* _____

_____
_____
_____
_____
_____
_____
_____
_____
_____
_____
_____
_____
_____
_____
_____
_____
_____
_____
_____
_____
_____
_____
_____
_____
_____
_____
_____
_____
_____
_____
_____
_____
_____
_____
_____
_____
_____

The Vision of the Proper One Accord
in the Church

Scripture Reading: Eph. 4:3-6; Matt. 18:19; Acts 1:14; 2:46; Rom. 15:5-6

Day 1

I. **The one accord in the church is the practice of the oneness of the Body, which is the oneness of the Spirit (Eph. 4:3-6):**

   A. From Ephesians 4:4-6 we can see that our practice of the oneness is based upon the attribute of the oneness of the church: one Spirit, one Lord, one God, one Body, one hope, one faith, one baptism.

   B. The practice of the genuine one accord in the church is the application of the oneness (Acts 1:14; 2:46).

   C. The practice of the oneness is with the one accord; when the oneness is practiced, it becomes the one accord:

      1. In John the Lord emphasized oneness, but in Acts the one accord is emphasized (John 10:30; 17:11, 21-23; Acts 1:14; 2:46; 4:24; 15:25).

      2. The landmark that divides the Gospels and the Acts is the one accord among the one hundred and twenty (1:14):

         a. The disciples had become one in the Body, and in that oneness they continued steadfastly with one accord in prayer (Eph. 4:3-6; Acts 1:14).

Day 2

         b. When the apostles and the believers practiced the church life, they practiced it in one accord (2:46; 4:24; 5:12).

      3. Oneness is like the physical body, and one accord is like the heart within the body:

         a. The one accord is the heart, the kernel, of the oneness.

         b. Our sickness is like a sickness in the heart within the body; the sickness among us is that we do not have the one accord adequately; therefore, we maintain only a oneness with a sick "heart."

D. Our not being in one accord means that we do not practice the Body:

   1. According to the proper interpretation of the New Testament, the one accord is the Body (Rom. 12:4-5; 15:5-6).

   2. We must practice the principle of the Body; then we will have the one accord (1 Cor. 12:12-13, 20, 27; 1:10).

Day 3   E. We are for the one accord, but we are not for uniformity (1 John 2:12-14):

   1. Any differences among the saints or the churches in the degree of the maturity of life are normal; we should not attempt to make the saints or the churches uniform in this matter, for in the degree of the growth in life, it is impossible to have uniformity (Phil. 3:15).

   2. Any differences among the saints or the churches that are intentional are abnormal and should be condemned and rejected.

II. **The one accord refers to the harmony in our inner being, in our mind and will (Acts 1:14):**

   A. In Acts 1:14 the Greek word *homothumadon* is used for *one accord:*

   1. The word denotes a harmony of inward feeling in one's entire being.

   2. We should be in the same mind and the same will with the same purpose around and within our soul and heart; this means that our entire being is involved.

Day 4   B. In Matthew 18:19 the Greek word *sumphoneo* is used to signify the one accord:

   1. The word means to be "in harmony, or accord" and refers to the harmonious sound of musical instruments or voices.

   2. The one accord, or the harmony of inward feeling among the believers, is like a harmonious melody.

3. When we have the one accord, we become a
melody to God; we become a poem not merely
in writing but in sound, in voice, in melody.

III. **Today we can be in one accord because we
have the same vision—the vision of the age
(Prov. 29:18a; Acts 26:19):**

A. Our vision should be one that matches the age, a
vision that includes everything that has gone
before us:

1. If our vision is not up to date, it will be impossible for us to be one.

2. Many love God and serve Him, but everyone
has his own vision; as a result, there is no way
to have the one accord.

3. As long as we have different views on a minor
point, we cannot have the one accord (Phil.
3:15).

4. The vision that matches the age is the vision
that extends all the way from Genesis to Revelation (Gen. 1:26; Rev. 21:2).

Day 5

B. We can be in one accord because we have one all-
inclusive vision:

1. The vision that the Lord has given His recovery
is an all-inclusive vision—the ultimate consummation of all the visions in the Bible, the New
Jerusalem; within this ultimate consummation everything is included (vv. 2, 10-11).

2. We all need to be in the up-to-date vision, having the same viewpoint.

IV. **The teaching of the apostles is the holding
factor of the one accord (Acts 2:42, 46):**

A. The proper one accord is according to the apostles'
teaching (v. 42).

B. Acts tells us that there was one accord among the
believers and that all those who were in one accord
continued steadfastly in the apostles' teaching.

C. The apostles taught the same thing to all the
saints in all the places and in all the churches
(1 Cor. 4:17; 7:17; 11:16; 14:33b-34):

Day 6

1. We also must teach the same thing in all the churches in every country throughout the earth (Matt. 28:19-20).

2. There is no thought in the New Testament that a teaching is good for one church but not for the other churches; rather, the New Testament reveals that all the churches were the same in receiving the teachings (Titus 1:9).

V. The one accord is the master key to every blessing in the New Testament (Eph. 1:3; Psa. 133):

A. We all want to see the church receive blessing; the commanded blessing of the Lord, which is life forever, is upon the brothers dwelling together in oneness.

B. The one accord is the way to bring in God's blessing; the blessing of God can come only upon a situation of one accord.

C. In order to receive God's blessing, we must practice the oneness, and the way to practice the oneness is to be in one accord (Eph. 4:4-6; Acts 1:14).

Morning Nourishment

Matt. Again, truly I say to you that if two of you are in har-
18:19 mony on earth concerning any matter for which
       they ask, it will be done for them from My Father
       who is in the heavens.
Acts These all continued steadfastly with one accord in
1:14 prayer...

Now we will consider the practice of oneness. Oneness is practiced through the one accord....The word *harmony* [in Matthew
18:19] in the original language, means to be in a musical harmony; this is the practice of oneness. By the time of Acts 1, there
were one hundred twenty people praying steadfastly in one
accord (vv. 14-15a). All of them had one mind, which was to
receive power from on high and to testify of the crucified, resurrected, and ascended Lord, whom they loved and followed. For
this they were in one mind, and were thus in one accord.

From Ephesians 4:4-6 we can see that our practice of oneness
is based upon the attribute of the oneness of the church: one
Spirit, one Lord, one God, one Body, one faith, one baptism, and
one hope. By this we can see that oneness is the attribute of the
church. Based upon this attribute of the oneness of the church, we
can be in one accord and can practice the oneness. (*The Oneness
and the One Accord according to the Lord's Aspiration and the
Body Life and Service according to His Pleasure*, pp. 16-17)

Today's Reading

In the Body we need oneness; in the churches and among the
churches, we need the one accord. The one accord is for our practice; the oneness is primarily for the actuality, for the fact. In
John 17 the Lord Jesus prayed for such a fact, and on the day of
Pentecost, by pouring out Himself as the consummated Spirit,
He accomplished His prayer. That was the actuality of the oneness. After the accomplishment of the actuality of the oneness,
there is the need for the practice of the oneness. When the oneness is practiced, it becomes the one accord. The one accord is
the practice of the oneness.

If we have only the oneness as an actuality, and do not have the present, practical one accord, the oneness that we have will be objective and abstract; it will not be real to us. If we would apply the oneness accomplished by the outpouring of the Spirit, we must practice the one accord....If in a prayer meeting we each pray in our own way, without any accord among us, how could we say that we are practicing the oneness? As long as we have differences existing among us, the oneness is not applied. We must have the one accord to swallow up all the differences; then oneness will be present.

The practice of the proper one accord in the church is the application of the oneness. Although oneness and one accord seem to be synonymous, there is a difference between them. The Lord did not teach us concerning oneness. In John 17 He prayed for oneness, but in Matthew 18 He led us to practice the one accord. In Matthew 18:19 the Lord spoke of two praying together on earth in one accord. That was His leading, His training, and His directing us to pray in one accord. (*The Intrinsic Problem in the Lord's Recovery Today and Its Scriptural Remedy*, pp. 23-24)

To have the home gatherings without the one accord means nothing. To go out to visit others to distribute the booklets needs the one accord. Without the one accord, all our doings will be in vain.

We must realize that the practices in the Lord's recovery are not matters for others to copy. You must have the life. To do anything you need the life. You have to see what the landmark was of the one hundred twenty in the book of Acts. The landmark that divides the Gospels and the Acts was not the baptism in the Holy Spirit. The landmark was the one accord of the one hundred twenty. If you want to experience the baptism in the Spirit, you must have the one accord. (*Elders' Training, Book 7: One Accord for the Lord's Move*, p. 18)

Further Reading: Elders' Training, Book 7: One Accord for the Lord's Move, ch. 1; The Intrinsic Problem in the Lord's Recovery Today and Its Scriptural Remedy, ch. 2

Enlightenment and inspiration: _____

_____

_____

_____

Morning Nourishment

Eph. Being diligent to keep the oneness of the Spirit in the
4:3-6 uniting bond of peace: one Body and one Spirit, even
       as also you were called in one hope of your calling;
       one Lord, one faith, one baptism; one God and Fath-
       er of all, who is over all and through all and in all.

The oneness that the Lord aspired for and prayed for in John 17 corresponds with the oneness of the Spirit in Ephesians 4:3-6. We must see that the church is the Body of Christ, which is a constitution, an entity constituted with the Triune God and His chosen and redeemed ones. In this Body there is the reality of oneness. The genuine oneness is not of the church but of the Body; the real oneness is the organic oneness of the Body. In a locality, this oneness is called *one accord*. Without the oneness of the Body, there is no possibility to have one accord in the church.

The one accord is first mentioned in Acts 1. The one hundred twenty had become one in the Body, and in that oneness they continued steadfastly with one accord in prayer (v. 14). (*The Governing and Controlling Vision in the Bible*, p. 29)

Today's Reading

Now we need to see the practice of the oneness, which is with one accord (Acts 1:14; 2:46; 4:24; 5:12; 15:25; Rom. 15:6). In the Gospel of John, the Lord stresses the oneness, but in the book of Acts, He stresses the one accord. Acts is not a book of teaching but a book of practice. When the apostles and the believers practiced the church life, they practiced it in one accord. To be in one accord is to be in harmony. When we practice the church life, we must practice being in harmony. To say "amen" to one another in our speaking for the Lord and in our pursuit of the Lord is to be in harmony. (*Messages to the Trainees in Fall 1990*, p. 124)

In a sense it is hard for the Lord to move freely among us. If we are not in one accord, God has no way to answer our prayer. If God does not have a way to answer our prayer, what can He do with us? Without the one accord, it is difficult to get people saved, converted, and regenerated by the dynamic salvation of God. Thus, our inadequacy in the one accord is a sickness that is more than serious. We have been sick for years, yet we might have been unconscious of our sickness. We may come to the meetings, praise the Lord, and prophesy, but we may do all these things without being conscious of the fact that we do not have the adequate one accord.

Although I have studied the Bible for many years, I did not see until recently that oneness is like the body, and one accord is like the heart within the body. Our sickness is not just like a sickness in the outward, physical body; our sickness is like a sickness in the heart within the body. I am speaking the truth frankly and honestly, according to what the Lord has shown me and according to my pure conscience. We need to know what our sickness is. The sickness among us is that we do not have the one accord adequately. Therefore, we maintain only a oneness with a sick "heart."

To build up the vital groups, we need to keep the oneness of the Spirit, that is, the oneness of the Body, in the one accord according to the Lord's desire with much and thorough prayer (Eph. 4:3; Acts 1:14; 4:24). Without the one accord we cannot keep the oneness. The one accord is the heart, the kernel, of the oneness.

If we do not have the one accord, God cannot answer our prayer, because we do not practice the Body. Our not being in one accord means that we do not practice the Body. According to the proper interpretation of the New Testament, the one accord is the one Body. We must practice the principle of the Body; then we will have the one accord. Although we may not fight with one another, we still may not have the one accord. Because we have remained together, we have seen the Lord's blessing, but only in a limited way. Therefore, we need to have the one accord to practice the Body. (*Fellowship concerning the Urgent Need of the Vital Groups,* pp. 77-78, 85, 89)

Further Reading: The Governing and Controlling Vision in the Bible, ch. 2; Messages to the Trainees in Fall 1990, ch. 17

Enlightenment and inspiration: _____

_____

_____

_____

Morning Nourishment

1 Cor. For even as the <u>body is one</u> and has <u>many mem-</u>
12:12 bers, yet all the members of the body, being <u>many</u>,
are <u>one</u> body, so also is the <u>Christ</u>.

1:10 Now I beseech you, brothers, through the name of
our Lord Jesus Christ, that you <u>all</u> speak the <u>same</u>
<u>thing</u> and *that* there be <u>no divisions</u> among you,
but *that* you be attuned in the <u>same mind</u> and in
the <u>same opinion</u>.

To <u>keep</u> the oneness, to <u>apply</u> the oneness, to <u>use</u> the oneness, to <u>enjoy</u> the oneness, to <u>spend</u> the oneness, we need to
<u>practice the one accord</u>. However, we should practice the one
accord not only among the saints in our particular locality; we
must practice the one accord among <u>all the churches</u> universally....We are <u>not for</u> uniformity among the churches, but we
are for oneness. (*Elders' Training, Book 10: The Eldership and
the God-ordained Way (2)*, p. 52)

Today's Reading

Uniformity and oneness are not the same thing. In a family
there may be a grandfather and a grandmother...a father and a
mother...and a number of children....They all are different in age,
different in the degree of maturity. In such a family it would be
impossible to make all the members uniformly the same age. However,...they can still be one. Likewise, in the church we do not
practice uniformity because in the household of God, a large household, there are many degrees of maturity among the children. To
eliminate the degrees of maturity would be absolutely wrong and
would be impossible. However, this does not mean that we do not
need oneness. In the practicality of the church life, as in the family
life, there is the need of oneness; but in the degree of the growth
in life, it is impossible to have uniformity.

Any differences among the saints or among the churches that
are intentional are abnormal and are condemned by the Scripture.
Any intention to have differences among the saints or among the
churches in order to demonstrate something or to oppose

something should be condemned and rejected. (*Elders' Training, Book 10: The Eldership and the God-ordained Way (2)*, pp. 52-53, 63-64)

In Acts 1:14 the one hundred twenty disciples prayed for ten days with one accord, and their prayer was answered in a marvelous way on the day of Pentecost. In this verse another Greek word, *homothumadon*, is used for "one accord." This word is from *homo*, meaning "same," and *thumos*, meaning "mind, will, purpose (soul, heart)." It denotes a harmony of inward feeling in one's entire being. The one accord is the expression and the application of the oneness. The harmony in Matthew 18:19 is the one accord in Acts 1:14. In Acts 1:14 one hundred twenty saints were praying in one accord. However, before that time they were not in one accord. Before the Lord's death the disciples contended with one another (Luke 22:24) and had no strength to pray (Matt. 26:40-45)....In the evening of the day of the Lord's resurrection, He came to the disciples and breathed into them the life-giving Spirit (John 20:22). This life-giving Spirit entered into the disciples essentially. This was the very dynamo that began to operate in them to bring them into one accord....The one accord among the saints is crucial for the carrying out of God's economy. (*1993 Blending Conference Messages concerning the Lord's Recovery and Our Present Need*, pp. 84-85)

Whenever we pray, we surely should exercise our spirit, but we also should be in the same mind and the same will with the same purpose around and within our soul and heart. This means that our entire being is involved. After the Lord's ascension, the one hundred twenty became the kind of persons who were in one mind, in one will, with one purpose around their soul and heart. For them to be in one accord meant that their entire beings were one. No other book of the Bible uses the word for "one accord" as much as Acts. (*Elders' Training, Book 7: One Accord for the Lord's Move*, pp. 10-11)

Further Reading: Elders' Training, Book 10: The Eldership and the God-ordained Way (2), ch. 4; 1993 Blending Conference Messages concerning the Lord's Recovery and Our Present Need, msg. 4

Enlightenment and inspiration: _____

_____

_____

_____

Morning Nourishment

Prov. Where there is no vision, the people cast off
29:18 restraint...
Acts Therefore, King Agrippa, I was not disobedient to
26:19 the heavenly vision.

Now we need to ask, what is the one accord? One accord
appears to be a less significant matter than oneness. Apparently,
oneness is a great thing, whereas one accord is a smaller matter.
It is easy to define oneness: oneness is the Triune God mingled
with all His believers, and this oneness is just the Body of Christ.
However, it is difficult to define one accord.

In Matthew 18:19 the Greek word *sumphoneo* is used for one
accord. It means "to be in harmony, or accord" and refers to the
harmonious sound of musical instruments or voices. Eventually,
the one accord, or the harmony of inward feeling among the
believers, becomes like a melody, like music. Every proper melody is harmonious. When we have the one accord, in the eyes of
God we become a melody to Him. We become a poem not merely
in writing but in sound, in voice, in melody. (*Fellowship concerning the Urgent Need of the Vital Groups*, p. 76)

Today's Reading

While you are serving the Lord, you should understand what
we are doing here. This is not a personal thing. It is absolutely
the Lord's ministry. He has unveiled the visions generation after
generation to His children. All those who are in this vision now
are serving according to God's vision.

Where there is no vision, the people cast off restraint, because
there is no one accord. It is true that many people love the Lord and
serve God, but everyone has his opinion and his own vision. As a result, there is no way to have the one accord. This is the reason that
Christianity has become so weak. God's people are divided and
split apart. There are divisions everywhere. Although everyone
says that he loves the Lord, there is no clear vision, and men are
"carried about by every wind" (Eph. 4:14).

Recently I have felt the importance of the one accord. As long as we have different views on a minor point, we cannot have the one accord. This is the reason that in this training, right from the beginning, I spoke concerning the vision in the Lord's recovery. I believe all the brothers and sisters love the Lord, and all of us want to be in one accord, but if our vision is not up to date, it is impossible for us to be one.

Our vision should be one that matches the age. It should also be one that includes everything that has gone before us. It should include the godliness of the Jews, the zeal of the evangelicals, and the genuine service. Only then will we be able to practice an all-inclusive church life, the church life Paul revealed to us (Rom. 14). We are not divided into sects, and we do not impose any special practice on anyone. We only live an all-inclusive church life. If we do this, we will have the genuine one accord.

Today we can be in one accord because we have only one vision and one view. We are all in this up-to-date, all-inheriting vision. We have only one viewpoint. We speak the same thing with one heart, one mouth, one voice, and one tone, serving the Lord together. The result is a power that will become our strong morale and our impact. This is our strength. Once the Lord's recovery possesses this power, there will be the glory of increase and multiplication. Today our situation is not yet to that point; it is not yet at the peak.

In the future I must give an account to the Lord. For this very reason I have observed the situation very much. Some emphasize the preaching of the cross, but there is not much practice with them. When they want to lose their temper, they still lose their temper. They do not preach the gospel, they do not nourish and perfect others, and they do not pursue after the truth. The cross is merely a doctrine to them. We do not care for mere doctrines. We need to see the vision. As we have seen, the vision that matches the age is the vision that extends all the way from Genesis to Revelation. (*The Vision of the Age*, pp. 53, 70, 54, 84)

Further Reading: Fellowship concerning the Urgent Need of the Vital Groups, msgs. 10, 12; The Vision of the Age, ch. 2

Enlightenment and inspiration: _____

_____

_____

_____

Morning Nourishment

Acts And they continued steadfastly in the teaching and
2:42 the fellowship of the apostles, in the breaking of
bread and the prayers.
46 And day by day, continuing steadfastly with one
accord in the temple and breaking bread from
house to house, they partook of *their* food with
exultation and simplicity of heart.

I would like the co-workers, the elders, and all the churches in
the Lord's recovery to realize that today we have not changed. If
we are different in any way from others, it is because we hold to all
the visions of the Bible, from the first vision of Adam in Genesis
to the ultimate, consummate one in Revelation. If anyone sees
only a part of this entire vision and condemns us for being different, it is not merely because we are different from them; it is
because they do not have the vision that matches the age.

Today the Lord has been merciful to His recovery. Within a
short period of sixty years, He has brought us to the ultimate consummation of all the visions. (*The Vision of the Age*, p. 81)

Today's Reading

I hope that all of us will seriously study the messages that we
have published, especially those in the *Elders' Training* and
Truth Lessons series. If we study them thoroughly, we will have
the full view; we will see the vision that the Lord has given us in
His recovery, and we will realize what is the ultimate consummation of all the visions—the New Jerusalem. Within this ultimate
consummation everything is included, such as gospel preaching,
loving the Lord, the dealing and breaking of the cross, the
resurrection life, and the outpouring of the Holy Spirit.

During the past nineteen hundred years, countless numbers of
Christians have been serving God....The Jews...also are serving
God. Of course, the Jews serve only according to the vision of the
Old Testament. Some Christians are serving according to the vi-
sion revealed in the New Testament Gospels, which has to do only
with the earthly ministry of Jesus. Some serve without any vision

at all....To serve God according to the up-to-date vision, we need to come up to the level of Paul's very last Epistles. In fact, we need to come up to the level of the epistles to the seven churches in Revelation as well as the revelation which covers all the ages, including the kingdom, the new heaven and new earth, and the ultimate consummation of the church—the New Jerusalem. Simply put, in order for us to serve God today, our vision must extend all the way from the first vision of Adam in Genesis to the ultimate vision of the manifestation of the church, the New Jerusalem. This and this alone is the complete vision. It is not until today that this vision has been fully opened to us. (*The Vision of the Age*, pp. 81-82, 48)

If you expect to have one accord in any kind of society, group, or movement, you need the same kind of thinking that comes out of the same kind of knowledge....Any society, group, or movement needs this one accord that comes out of the same kind of thought, the same kind of knowledge. Therefore, Acts tells us that on the one hand, there was one accord among the disciples, and on the other hand, all those who were one in one accord were continuing in the teaching of the apostles (2:42). The teaching of the apostles was the very holding factor of the one accord. If there were more than one teaching, this would damage the holding factor. (*Elders' Training, Book 7: One Accord for the Lord's Move*, p. 100)

The apostles taught the same thing to all the saints in all the places and in all the churches. At the same time, the practice of this oneness is also according to the same speaking of the Spirit to the churches (Rev. 2:7, 11a, 17a, 29; 3:6, 13, 22). The seven epistles to the seven churches in Revelation 2 and 3 were words spoken to all the churches. He who has an ear, let him hear. Each epistle was written to all the churches. All the churches have the same Bible, and everyone is practicing oneness according to the same speaking. (*The Oneness and the One Accord according to the Lord's Aspiration and the Body Life and Service according to His Pleasure*, pp. 17-18)

Further Reading: The Vision of the Age, ch. 3; Elders' Training, Book 7: One Accord for the Lord's Move, ch. 8

Enlightenment and inspiration: _____

_____

_____

_____

Morning Nourishment

Psa. Behold, how good and how pleasant it is for broth-
133 ers to dwell in unity! It is like the fine oil upon the
head that ran down upon the beard, upon Aaron's
beard, that ran down upon the hem of his gar-
ments; like the dew of Hermon that came down
upon the mountains of Zion. For there Jehovah
commanded the blessing: life forever.

All of us need to be one with the Lord in the life pulse of His new
move. For the Lord's new move, all of the churches need to be in one
accord. In the past, we lost the one accord, but we must endeavor to
recover and keep it. We also must teach the same thing in all the
churches in every country throughout the earth. There should be
no different trumpeting or different voicing among us. We should
all voice the same thing, trumpet the same thing, and teach the
same thing. We need to be one in teaching. (*Elders' Training, Book
9: The Eldership and the God-ordained Way (1)* p. 16)

Today's Reading

All the churches are the same in receiving the teachings of the
apostles. In 1 Corinthians 4:17b Paul says, "Even as I teach everywhere in every church." This indicates that the apostles' teaching is
the same universally, not varying in any place. In...7:17 Paul says,
"However as the Lord has apportioned to each one, as God has
called each one, so let him walk. And so I direct in all the churches."
This is a further indication that all the churches were the same in
receiving Paul's teachings. In 1 Corinthians 16:1 Paul goes on to
say, "Now concerning the collection for the saints, just as I directed
the churches of Galatia, so you also do." Here Paul instructed the
church in Corinth to do what he had directed the churches of Galatia to do. This is a further indication that all the churches under
Paul's ministry were one in the apostles' teaching (Acts 2:42).

Some who do not realize that all the churches should be the
same in receiving the apostles' teachings may think that a certain
teaching is good for one church but not for their church. To have
this attitude is to be closed to the fellowship among the churches.

Any teaching that is good for a particular church is good for all the churches on earth. Likewise, if a teaching is not good for a particular church, it should be rejected by all the churches. There is no thought in the New Testament that a teaching is good for one church but not for the other churches. Rather, the New Testament reveals that the churches should be the same in receiving the teachings. (*The Conclusion of the New Testament,* pp. 2187-2188)

If you really want to practice the proper way to preach the gospel, you need the one accord. Without this key, no door can be opened. The one accord is the "master key to all the rooms," the master key to every blessing in the New Testament. This is why Paul told Euodias and Syntyche that they needed this one accord (Phil. 4:2). Paul knew that these sisters loved the Lord, but that they had lost the one accord.

What we need is to recover this one accord. If we mean business to go along with the Lord's present day move, we need this one accord. Who is right does not mean anything; we need this one accord. We need to have the same mind and the same will for the same purpose with the same soul and the same heart. (*Elders' Training, Book 7: One Accord for the Lord's Move,* pp. 18-19)

We must be in one accord to maintain the oneness Christ seeks. Since we are bearing the responsibility of the church, we should see the way for the church to receive grace and blessing. We must all realize that the blessing and grace of God can only come upon a situation of one accord. This situation is the practice of oneness. In the Old Testament, Psalm 133 says, "Behold, how good and how pleasant it is / For brothers to dwell in unity!…For there Jehovah commanded the blessing: / Life forever." God will only grace and bless the one accord, that is, the practice of oneness. (*The Oneness and the One Accord according to the Lord's Aspiration and the Body Life and Service according to His Pleasure,* p. 18)

Further Reading: The Conclusion of the New Testament, msg. 204;
   The Oneness and the One Accord according to the Lord's Aspiration and the Body Life and Service according to His Pleasure, ch. 1

Enlightenment and inspiration: _____

_____

_____

_____

Hymns, #1108

1   Eat the bread, ye people of the Lord:
Praise His name, for He has made us one.
Now we come to eat in one accord
As the church which He has made His own.

    Eat the bread and drink the wine, ye saints!
We are one in Him fore'er.
Stand in oneness on the local ground,
Eat and drink in oneness there!

2   Drink the wine, ye people of the Lord:
We're the church His precious blood has bought.
We're redeemed to be in one accord —
This the goal for which He long has sought.

3   Stand as one, ye people of the Lord:
Not as individual grains are we —
We are one, we're blent in one accord
As a loaf in each locality.

4   We are one as people of the Lord;
We declare that we are really one!
Not just word, but life in one accord
Testify what God in us hath done.

5   Eat the bread, ye people of the Lord:
Praise His name, for He has made us one.
Now we come to eat in one accord
As the church which He has made His own.

    (Do not repeat chorus after last verse)

Composition for prophecy with main point and sub-points: _____

_____
_____
_____
_____
_____
_____
_____
_____
_____
_____
_____
_____
_____
_____
_____
_____
_____
_____
_____
_____
_____
_____
_____
_____
_____
_____
_____
_____
_____
_____
_____
_____
_____
_____

WEEK 4 — OUTLINE

Teach me O Jehovah, Your way
I will walk in Your truth
Make my heart single

The Practice of the Proper One Accord in the Church

(Psa 86:11-12)

Scripture Reading: Rom. 15:5-6; 1 Cor. 1:10; Phil. 1:27; Jer. 32:39

Day 1

2: Paul & Bob

I. **If we would be in one accord, we must learn to be in one spirit with one soul (Phil. 1:27):**

1: Warren & Harold

A. We need to turn to our spirit and then enter into our soul with one spirit so that we may be in one accord (v. 27; 2:2, 5; 4:2).

B. The secret of experiencing Christ is to be like-souled in the Body life, genuinely caring for the things of Christ Jesus (1:27; 2:21):

1. If we would experience Christ to the fullest extent in the Body and for the Body, we need to be like-souled (vv. 2, 19-20).

2. Because Timothy was like-souled with Paul, he was in the position to experience Christ to the uttermost in the Body (1 Cor. 4:16-17; 16:10).

Day 2

1: Carla, Kevin's

II. **In order to practice the one accord, we should "be attuned in the same mind and in the same opinion" (1:10):**

2: Sally & Jarvis

A. The problem in the church life that keeps us from realizing the one accord is our opinion (Matt. 16:22-25; Phil. 2:2; 4:2).

B. In the Lord's work, in the church life, and in the spiritual life, the greatest damaging factor is our opinion (1 Cor. 1:10-13a).

C. Our usefulness before the Lord depends greatly on the matter of opinion (7:25, 40).

D. The Corinthian believers needed to be mended in order to be perfectly joined together so that they might be in harmony, having the same mind and the same opinion to speak the same thing—Christ and His cross (1:10, 17-19, 22-24; 2:2).

III. **If we would have the proper one accord in the church life, we need to be of the same mind and think the same thing, the one thing (Rom.**

2: (Frank Jenny)

1: (Jean & Ken)

12:16; 15:5; Phil. 2:2; 4:2):

A. The entire Bible has one mouth and speaks the same thing (Heb. 1:1-2a).

B. In the church life we all need to take Christ as our person in the matter of speaking (Matt. 12:34-37; Eph. 3:17a; John 7:16-18; 8:28, 38a; 12:49-50; 14:10).

Day 3

C. If we all take Christ as our person and as our life, spontaneously we will all speak the same thing (Eph. 3:17a; Col. 3:4; 1 Cor. 1:10).

D. *With one accord* and *with one mouth* (Rom. 15:6) mean that even though we are many and all are speaking, we all "speak the same thing" (1 Cor. 1:10):

1. The church is the one new man with only one person—Christ—and this person controls our speaking; thus, whatever He speaks is surely "the same thing."

2. When we are about to speak, we need to resolve a basic question: in this matter of speaking, am I the person or is Christ the person?

3. If in our speaking we do not take ourselves as the person but allow Christ to be the person, then there will be one mouth, and everyone will speak the same thing.

Day 4

E. To be in one accord is to be one in our whole being, and this results in our being one in our outward speaking (Rom. 15:5-6):

1. To have one mind and one mouth means that we have only one Head—Christ—because only the Head has a mind and a mouth; we should think with the mind of Christ and speak with the mouth of the Head (Col. 1:18a; Phil. 2:2, 5; 4:2).

2. Whenever we are in one accord, we speak the same thing; we speak with one mouth.

3. The only way to be with one accord and one mouth is to allow Christ the room to be everything in our heart and in our mouth so that God may be glorified (Eph. 3:17a, 21).

Day 5

IV. **If we would be in one accord, we need to have one heart and one way (Jer. 32:39):**

    A. Believers are divided because they take many different ways other than Christ (John 14:6; 1 Cor. 1:30).

    B. We, the chosen people of God, should all have one heart—to love God, to seek God, to live God, and to be constituted with God so that we may be His expression—and one way—the Triune God Himself as our inner law of life with its divine capacity (Mark 12:30; Jer. 31:33-34; John 14:6a).

    C. This one heart and one way are the one accord (Acts 1:14; 2:46; Rom. 15:6).

    D. Divisions result from having a heart for something other than Christ and taking a way other than Christ.

V. **In order to be in one accord, we should have only one "scale" in the church life (Deut. 25:13-16):**

    A. The dishonest practice of having differing weights and measures is a lie and is surely from Satan (John 8:44).

    B. In spiritual application, to condemn a certain thing in others while justifying the same thing in ourselves indicates that we have different weights and measures, that is, different scales—one scale for measuring others and a different scale for measuring ourselves.

Day 6

    C. In the house of God, the church (1 Tim. 3:15), only one scale should be used to weigh everyone.

    D. The practice of having different scales is the source of discord; instead of keeping the oneness and the one accord, we have discord.

    E. We all need to receive mercy from the Lord to no longer have differing scales but, like our God, to have the same scale for everyone.

    F. If we have only one scale, we will keep the oneness and have the real one accord in the church (Eph. 4:1-3; Matt. 7:1-5).

    G. If we have only one "scale," we will be fair, just, and righteous, even as God is, and we will keep the oneness and the one accord in the church.

VI. **For the Lord's up-to-date move, all the churches need to be in one accord (Josh. 1:16-18; 6:1-16):**
   A. We should all voice the same thing, trumpet the same thing, and teach the same thing (1 Cor. 4:17; 7:17; 16:1; Acts 2:42; Rom. 16:17; 1 Tim. 1:4-5; 6:3).
   B. All the churches should also be the same in practice; if the churches are not the same in practice, this will damage the one accord (1 Cor. 11:16).
   C. In the Lord's recovery, and especially in His up-to-date move, we must see that the crucial need today is the recovery of the one accord (Acts 1:14).

Morning Nourishment

Phil. Only, conduct yourselves in a manner worthy of the
1:27 gospel of Christ, that whether coming and seeing you
or being absent, I may hear of the things concerning
you, that you stand firm in one spirit, with one soul
striving together *along* with the faith of the gospel.
2:2 Make my joy full, that you think the same thing,
having the same love, joined in soul, thinking the
one thing.

When we practice the one accord, we must learn to be in one
spirit and with one soul (Phil. 1:27). We may be bodily sitting
together in the same room, but if we are not one in our spirit, it is
certain that we will not be one in our soul. To practice the one
accord, we must learn to turn to our spirit and then to enter into
our soul with the spirit that we may be in the one accord. (*Elders'
Training, Book 10: The Eldership and the God-ordained Way (2)*, p. 54)

Today's Reading

The book of Philippians deals very much with the soul of
believers. We must strive together with one soul in the faith of the
gospel (1:27); we must be joined in soul, thinking the one thing
(2:2); and we must be like-souled, genuinely caring for the things
of the Lord (2:20-21). In the gospel work, in the fellowship among
the believers, and in the Lord's interests, our soul is always a
problem. Hence, it must be transformed, especially in its leading
part, the mind (Rom. 12:2), that we may be of one soul, joined in
soul, and like-souled in the Body life.

In the book of Philippians the experience of Christ is the key
point, and the secret of the experience of Christ is to be one in soul
or joined in soul. According to this book, we cannot go on in the
experience of Christ unless we are joined in soul. If we are one
only in spirit but are not joined in soul, we cannot go on in the
experience of Christ.

There is a great difference between being in the soul and being
one in soul or joined in soul. The secret of experiencing Christ is to

be one in soul, not to be in the soul. The dissenting ones who are al-together in the soul find it impossible to be one in soul. Those who exercise their mind, emotion, and will are not one in soul. If we would experience Christ, we need to be one with others in the soul; that is, we need to become like-souled with others. When we exercise our mind, emotion, and will, we may be very individualistic. But if we exercise our spirit to be one in soul, our mind will be sobered, our emotion will be regulated, and our will will be adjusted. Then it will be possible for us to be one in soul with other saints.

Paul's word about being like-souled is a warning to all who remain in the Lord's recovery. If we are not like-souled with others, we shall not have the full enjoyment of Christ, even though we stay in the church life. Although we have no problems in our spirit, we may hold on to differences in our soul. According to your impression, the feeling you have in your soul is right. However, because you hold on to your differences, your experience of Christ is limited. Thus, it is crucial for us all to learn that in the church life we need to be like-souled. Do not allow the differences in your soul to hold you back from experiencing Christ in His Body. May we all learn to sacrifice our soul, to risk our mind, emotion, and will. Then we shall become like-souled with others in the Body of Christ. If this is our condition, how much we shall experience Christ and enjoy Him in the Body! In order to experience Christ to the full extent in the Body, we need to be like-souled and we need to risk our soul.

Any co-worker who could not be sent by Paul with such a concern for the Body of Christ could not experience Christ to the same degree Paul did. Because Timothy was like-souled with Paul, he was in a position to experience Christ to the uttermost in the Body, just as Paul was experiencing Him. But those who were different in soul from Paul could not experience Christ to this high degree. Their experience of Christ was restricted by the differences in soul. (*Life-study of Philippians,* pp. 125-126, 137-138, 134-135)

Further Reading: Life-study of Philippians, msgs. 2, 8

Enlightenment and inspiration: _____

_____

_____

_____

Morning Nourishment

1 Cor. Now I beseech you, brothers, through the name of our
1:10 Lord Jesus Christ, that you all speak the same thing
and *that* there be no divisions among you, but *that* you
be attuned in the same mind and in the same opinion.
Phil. I exhort Euodias, and I exhort Syntyche, to think the
4:2 same thing in the Lord.

The proper one accord in the church is the practice of the genuine oneness of the Body (Matt. 18:19; Acts 1:14). In Matthew
18:19, before the Lord prayed for the oneness in John 17, He
trained His disciples to practice the one accord.

To practice the one accord, we must be attuned in the same
mind and in the same opinion (1 Cor. 1:10). To be attuned in the
same mind is to practically be one in our soul. When the thoughts
in our mind are expressed in our speaking, they become our opinions. When the opinions remain in our mind, they are simply our
thoughts. When our differences in thinking are expressed as
opinions, that may cause a problem.

The Corinthian believers were not attuned in the same mind;
thus, they spoke differently in the flesh. Some said, "I am of Paul,"
and others, "I am of Apollos" or "I am of Cephas" (1 Cor. 1:12). The
supposedly spiritual ones among them said, "I am of Christ." This
too was the expressing of an opinion. This kind of different speaking caused divisions among the Corinthians. (*Elders' Training,
Book 10: The Eldership and the God-ordained Way (2)*, pp. 53-54)

Today's Reading

In marriage life the sin of ambition does not arise every day,
but the problem of opinion may arise many times each day. Both
brothers and sisters have their opinions....When a brother is
driving a car, his wife may express many opinions about the way
to drive, but the husband may silently carry out his own opinion.

In the Lord's work, in the church life, and in the spiritual life,
the greatest damaging factor is our opinion. For many years in the
Lord's work I have seen the problem of opinion. Our usefulness before the Lord depends greatly on the matter of our opinion. If we

are opinionated, we are through with the Lord's work.

Apparently, the Christian life is an individual matter. Nevertheless, how much we grow in life also depends upon our opinion. How much growth we have had since we were saved has depended upon how we have dealt with our opinion. Opinion is a great matter. It is within us like the marrow in our bones. If the Lord tells us to go see a certain sister, we may say that we are not ready. This is our opinion. (*The Experience and Growth in Life*, pp. 142-143)

First Corinthians 1:10 speaks of being attuned in the same mind and in the same opinion. [Footnote 4 says that] the word *attuned* [is]…"the same word in Greek that is translated *mending* in Matthew 4:21. It means *to repair, to restore, to adjust, to mend, making a broken thing thoroughly complete, joined perfectly together.* The Corinthian believers as a whole were divided, broken. They needed to be mended in order to be joined perfectly together that they might be in harmony, having the same mind and the same opinion to speak the same thing, that is, Christ and His cross." To be attuned is to be joined together, as a piano is tuned to give a proper harmony and melody. Learn to be attuned, learn to be adjusted, and learn to be corrected. (*A Word of Love to the Co-workers, Elders, Lovers, and Seekers of the Lord*, p. 58)

Consider the Bible. The Old and New Testaments contain sixty-six books written by more than forty different authors in many different places over a period of fifteen or sixteen hundred years. The first book, Genesis, was written about 1500 B.C., while the last book, Revelation, was written after A.D. 90….The entire Bible has one mouth and speaks the same thing, even though it was written over a long period of time by many different people in many different places. Now you can understand what it means to have one mouth speaking the same thing. (*One Body, One Spirit, and One New Man*, pp. 59-60)

Further Reading: The Experience and Growth in Life, msg. 22; A Word of Love to the Co-workers, Elders, Lovers, and Seekers of the Lord, ch. 4

Enlightenment and inspiration: _____

_____

_____

_____

Morning Nourishment

Rom. Now the God of endurance and encouragement grant
15:5-6 you to be of the same mind toward one another
according to Christ Jesus, that with one accord you
may with one mouth glorify the God and Father of
our Lord Jesus Christ.

Years ago these verses [in Romans 15:5-6] bothered me. How
could tens of thousands of believers speak the same thing with
one mind and one mouth? Today I have the full assurance, not
merely doctrinally but experientially, that we all can speak the
same thing because the same thing which we speak is the all-
inclusive Christ. What we speak is not concerning baptisms,
head covering, or foot-washing. We speak one thing—the all-
inclusive Christ and His church. If we only take Christ as our life
and Christ as our person, spontaneously we will all speak the
same thing. Then practically we will be the new man. When you
go to another country, a saint there will meet you, speaking the
same thing. Wherever you go on the earth,...you will hear
the same thing. We all can speak the same thing, and we can all
be attuned in the same opinion. We would only have one concept,
Christ and the church. (*The One New Man,* p. 43)

Today's Reading

The church is not merely the Body but also the one new man. The
Body needs Christ as its life, whereas the new man needs Christ
as his person. When you want to speak, when I want to speak,
when any one of us wants to speak, we must resolve the basic
question: Who is the person that is speaking here? If you are the
person, you have your own mouth. If I am the person, I have my
own mouth. Thus, you have your mouth, and I have my mouth;
therefore, there are two mouths. When each one is a person indi-
vidually and each one speaks his own matters, we have many
mouths. This is a society or a denomination, and this is the condition of today's degraded Christianity. In the Lord's recovery,
however, the church is the Body, and the church is the one new
man. The Body has Christ as life, and the new man has Christ as

a person. When you speak, it is not you who are the person; when I speak, neither is it I. When anyone speaks, it is Christ who is the person. What is the result? The result is that there is only one mouth.

This is why in 1 Corinthians 1:10 Paul says that all "speak the same thing." This verse greatly bothered me many years ago. I thought, "How could all Christians speak the same thing?" It seemed to me that this was impossible, but one day I understood. The church is the one new man with only one person, and this person controls our speaking, so whatever He speaks is surely "the same thing" that we all speak as the new man.

Many preachers and pastors in today's Christianity are all their own persons, all have their own mouths, and all speak their own things. Therefore, they have many mouths, each speaking a different thing. However, the church is not like this. The church is the one new man with Christ as her person. Whenever the brothers and sisters are about to speak something, they do not take themselves as the person; instead, they allow Christ to be the person. You let Christ be your person when you speak, and I let Christ be my person when I speak. Eventually, everyone speaks the same thing.

Dear brothers and sisters, what I have fellowshipped with you here is something that I know. Many times I wanted to speak, but I checked within, asking myself, "Is it I who want to speak or is it the Lord?" In other words, in the matter of speaking, is the Lord the person, or am I the person? If it is I, there will be a problem; if it is the Lord, there will be no problem. If I allow the Lord to be the person, He is the One who speaks; then two months later, if you allow the Lord to be the person, you will speak the same thing that I have spoken. We have one mouth speaking the same thing. (*One Body, One Spirit, and One New Man*, pp. 59-60)

Further Reading: The One New Man, chs. 3-4; *One Body, One Spirit, and One New Man*, ch. 5

Enlightenment and inspiration: _____

_____

_____

_____

Morning Nourishment

Eph. That Christ may make His home in your hearts
3:17 through faith, that you, being rooted and grounded
in love.
   21 To Him be the glory in the church and in Christ Jesus
unto all the generations forever and ever. Amen.

[In Romans 15:6] the Greek word [for "with one accord"] means *with the same mind, will, and purpose.* This is to be one in our whole being and results in our being one in our outward speaking. Whenever we are in one accord, we speak the same thing; we speak with one mouth. This oneness is the reverse of Babel, where the division among mankind caused their language to become confused and divided into many different speakings (Gen. 11:7, 9). The only way to be with one accord and one mouth is to allow Christ the room to be everything in our heart and in our mouth that God may be glorified. (Rom. 15:6, footnote 1)

Today's Reading

We need to have one mind and one mouth. This means that we only have one Head because only the head has a mouth and a mind. We all take the Lord Jesus as the Head. Only He is fully qualified to have the mind and to have the mouth. We do not have the right because we are members of the Body. We do not have the mouth or the mind so we have to think with the mind of Christ (Phil 2:2, 5; 4:2). Then we have to speak with the mouth of the Head. The mouth only has one head.

If we considered this matter, we would not speak so loosely or freely; we would not speak whatever we like. You may like to speak something which the Head does not like. You are not the mouth. In the whole universe there is only one new man, and the one new man only has one Head with one Body. The mouth is not on the Body but with the Head. We must learn not to speak things so easily. Your speaking interferes with or profanes the mouth of the Head. You do not have any mouth. What the church has as the mouth is the mouth of the Head.

What does it mean that we all have one mind and one mouth?

This means "it is no longer I...but it is Christ who lives in me" (Gal. 2:20a). It is no more I, but Christ the Head that lives in me. He has a mouth, He has a mind, and I take Him as my person, so I would never use my mouth any longer to speak anything. Who could believe that so many millions of Christians with different languages could have one mouth? The Bible tells us this and we need to practice the one mouth to be one in speaking. (*Elders' Training, Book 7: One Accord for the Lord's Move*, pp. 44-45)

The Body is a matter of being members one of another, but for the new man the requirements are even more than what the Body requires....How many mouths does a man have? It has one. Not only are we all members one of another, but we also all speak with one mouth. Do you see how much is required of us? It is already restricting enough to be members one of another, and now even when we speak, we all have to have one mouth. This is not my word; it is Paul's word. How many mouths does the one new man have? One. Then who is the mouth? If you say that Christ is the mouth, you are too transcendent. In order to resolve this matter you must see that there is only one new man with only one person. In the whole body there is only one mouth, but who controls this mouth? It is the person who controls the mouth. (*One Body, One Spirit, and One New Man*, pp. 58-59)

We need to be of the same mind toward one another according to Christ Jesus so that with one accord we may glorify God in receiving the believers to live the church life (Rom. 15:5-7). Whenever we are in one accord, we speak the same thing; we speak with one mouth. The only way to be with one accord and with one mouth is to allow Christ the room to be everything in our heart and in our mouth that God may be glorified. We have said that God is the New Jerusalem. When we glorify God, we take Him as the New Jerusalem and give all the glory to Him. (*The Experience of God's Organic Salvation Equaling Reigning in Christ's Life*, p. 63)

Further Reading: Elders' Training, Book 7: One Accord for the Lord's Move, chs. 3-4

Enlightenment and inspiration: _____

_____

_____

_____

Morning Nourishment

Jer. **And I will give them** <u>one heart</u> **and** <u>one way</u>**, to fear**
32:39 **Me all the days, for their own good and for** *the good*
of **their children after them.**

John **Jesus said to him, I am the** <u>way</u> **and the reality and the**
14:6 **life; no one comes to the Father except through Me.**

According to Jeremiah 32:38, Israel would be Jehovah's people, and He would be their God. After making this promise, Jehovah said, "I will give them one heart and one way, to fear Me all the days, for their own good and for the good of their children after them" (v. 39).

We, the chosen people of God, should all have one heart and one way. We should have one heart to love God, to seek God, to live God, and to be constituted with God. This means that we love to be the expression of God. The one way is just the Triune God. The Lord Jesus said, "I am the way" (John 14:6a). (*Life-study of Jeremiah*, pp. 188-189)

Today's Reading

Christians today are divided because they take many different ways other than Christ. The Catholic Church has the Catholic way, and the Orthodox Church has the Orthodox way. Each denomination and independent group has its own way. The Presbyterians have one way, and the Pentecostals have another way.

What should be our way in the Body of Christ? As the Body of Christ, we should take the way of the inner law, which is the Triune God with His divine capacity. We should all have one heart to love Him, and we should all take Him as our life and our way. This one heart and one way is the one accord (Acts 1:14). If we do not have one heart and one way, we cannot be in one accord.

For eternity in the New Jerusalem there will be only one way. John tells us, "He showed me a river of water of life, bright as crystal, proceeding out of the throne of God and of the Lamb in the middle of its street. And on this side and on that side of the river was the tree of life, producing twelve fruits, yielding its fruit each month" (Rev. 22:1-2a). In the middle of the street, the river of water of life flows, and in the river the tree of life grows. This indicates that the way, the life, and the life supply are all one. It also indicates what our way should be today. Our way in the Lord's recovery is life; it is the inner law of life; it is the very Triune God Himself.

I am sorry to say that in recent years there was a turmoil among us, and this turmoil brought in division. The reason for this turmoil was that certain ones wanted to take a way other than life, a way other than Christ, the Triune God, and the inner law. Divisions are always the result of taking a way other than Christ. If we keep ourselves to the one way, there will be no division. We praise the Lord that in His restoration He will give His people one heart to love Him and express Him and one way to enjoy Him. (*Life-study of Jeremiah,* pp. 189-190)

Deuteronomy 25:13-16 covers the judgment concerning weights and measures. The children of Israel were not to have in their bag differing weights, one heavy and one light, nor were they to have in their house differing measures, one heavy and one light (vv. 13-14). For everyone who did these things, everyone who did unrighteousness, was an abomination to Jehovah their God (v. 16).

To have differing weights and measures is a lie, and all lies come from the enemy, Satan. The dishonest practice of having differing weights and measures is surely from Satan.

The children of Israel were to have a full and righteous weight and a full and righteous measure in order that their days might be extended upon the God-given land (v. 15). Here longevity is related to righteousness. Those who have lived a long life often attribute their longevity to such matters as taking care of their health, getting adequate sleep, and having a proper diet. Have you ever heard anyone attribute longevity to being fair, righteous, and just? In this verse living long upon the land is clearly related to having full and righteous weights and measures. (*Life-study of Deuteronomy,* p. 134)

Further Reading: Life-study of Jeremiah, msg. 27; *Life-study of Romans,* msg. 29*

Enlightenment and inspiration: _____

_____

_____

_____

Morning Nourishment

Deut. A full and righteous weight you shall have, *and* a
25:15 full and righteous measure you shall have, in order
that your days may be extended upon the land which
Jehovah your God is giving you.

1 Cor. ...I have sent Timothy to you,...who will remind
4:17 you of my ways which are in Christ, even as I teach
everywhere in every church.

Those who have differing weights and measures actually
have differing scales. In the church life today, we may have differing scales—one scale for measuring others and a different
scale for measuring ourselves. Having differing scales, we may
condemn a certain thing in others but justify the same thing in
ourselves. Certain saints may use one scale to weigh the actions
of the elders and the co-workers but a different scale in weighing
their own actions. Because they weigh the elders and co-workers
in one scale and themselves in a different scale, they find fault
with the elders and co-workers but vindicate themselves.

In the house of God, the church, there should be only one
scale. This means that the same scale should be used to weigh
everyone. If we have only one scale, we will be fair, righteous, and
just, even as God is. Because God is fair, righteous, and just, He
measures everyone according to the same scale. He does not
have differing weights or measures. For eternity He will use the
same scale. (*Life-study of Deuteronomy,* pp. 134-135)

Today's Reading

Because people use many different kinds of scales, there is a
great shortage of justice in human society. For instance, wives and
husbands use different scales in their married life. These different
scales are the reason for the quarreling between husband and wife.
Both the husband and wife have two sets of scales.

Although we should not have differing scales in the church
life, one scale for weighing ourselves and other scales for weighing
the brothers and sisters, we all have failed in this matter. Not one
of us is an exception. Using the language of accounting, we may

say that it is easy for us to "debit" others and "credit" ourselves. Instead of doing this, we should give others more credit and ourselves more debit. For instance, a sister may weigh the elders in one scale, giving them a debit, and weigh herself in a differing scale, giving herself a credit. If she would give the elders more credit and give herself more debit, she would have a much more positive view of the elders and of the church in her locality.

Some saints who have the practice of using differing scales may move from one locality to another, hoping to find a more satisfactory church with more satisfactory elders. But because these saints have differing scales, no matter where they may go, they do not find the church and the elders to be satisfactory.

I emphasize the practice of having differing scales because this practice is a sickness, a disease, in the church life. This is the source of disaccord. Instead of keeping the oneness and the one accord, we have disaccord. May we all receive mercy from the Lord to no longer have differing scales but, like our God, to have the same scale for everyone. (*Life-study of Deuteronomy,* pp. 135-136)

All of the churches should also be one in practice (1 Cor. 11:16; 14:33b-34). If the churches are not the same in practice, this will damage the one accord. If we train the full-timers in the God-ordained way, and they return to churches who practice differently, this could cause problems. We will be contradicting ourselves. I hope that all the trainees who return to their churches will be so useful because we are all practicing the same way.

In the early days of the church life, the churches were the same in practice. When Paul went to Jerusalem, however, he saw something different (Acts 21:20; see James 2:10 and footnote 1...). Eventually, the Lord wiped out that different thing in Jerusalem....In the Lord's recovery, there should only be one work in one move with one ministry for the building up of the one Body. (*Elders' Training, Book 9: The Eldership and the God-ordained Way (1),* pp. 16-17)

Further Reading: Life-study of Deuteronomy, msg. 19; *Elders' Training, Book 10: The Eldership and the God-ordained Way (2),* ch. 5

Enlightenment and inspiration: _____

_____

_____

_____

Hymns, #1243

1   We are one in the spirit, by His life we are one,
    We have left all divisions, Body-life has begun,
    For the Lord broke all barriers, proclaiming,
      "It is done."

> *Brothers:*
>   In the church we are brothers,
>   Praise the Lord, praise the Lord!

> *Sisters:*
>   In the church we are sisters,
>   Praise the Lord, praise the Lord!
>   (Praise the Lord!)

> *Everyone:*
>   And we praise Him that our unity
>   has now been restored.

2   We are one in the spirit, yet it goes deeper still,
    For this oneness is spreading to our mind, emotion, will,
    As we all stand together that His purpose
      He fulfill.

3   We are one in the spirit, we are one actually,
    Not in talk nor in theory, but in fact, practically,
    In the churches we're all enjoying this
      reality.

4   We are one in the spirit in each locality,
    For the Lord's own intention we would consecrated be,
    That the oneness He's given us the whole world
      may see.

Composition for prophecy with main point and sub-points: _____

_____
_____
_____
_____
_____
_____
_____
_____
_____
_____
_____
_____
_____
_____
_____
_____
_____
_____
_____
_____
_____
_____
_____
_____
_____
_____
_____
_____
_____
_____
_____
_____
_____
_____
_____

God's move is to deify man

The Lord's Move Today

Scripture Reading: Matt. 16:18; Rom. 15:16; 1 Pet. 2:5; Acts 5:42; Eph. 4:12; 1 Cor. 14:1, 3-5, 26, 31

Day 1

I. Our God is living (1 Tim. 3:15; Heb. 3:12), our Lord is moving (Matt. 16:18), the Spirit is working (Rev. 5:6b), and the people who know their God will show strength and take action (Dan. 11:32).

II. The Lord's move today is for His people to enter into a new revival:

A. Among God's elect there has always been an aspiration to be revived (Hab. 3:2a; Hosea 6:2; Rom. 8:20-22).

B. We can enter into a new revival by arriving at the highest peak of the divine revelation through the ministry of the age:

1. The highest peak of the divine revelation given to us by God is the revelation of the eternal economy of God.

2. The entire Bible, which is the explanation of the eternal economy of God, is the autobiography of the Triune God, seen in the two sections of eternity and on the bridge of time (John 1:1, 3, 14, 29, 32, 42, 51).

3. God becoming man that man might become God in life and in nature but not in the Godhead is the essence of the entire Bible, the "diamond" in the "box" of the Bible, the eternal economy of God (Gen. 1:26; John 12:24; Rom. 8:29).

4. In every age there is the vision of that age, and we have to serve God according to the vision of the age; today we can be in one accord because we have only one vision, an up-to-date, all-inheriting vision, the vision of the eternal economy of God (Prov. 29:18a; Acts 26:19; Eph. 1:17; 3:9).

5. "I hope that the saints in all the churches

throughout the earth, especially the co-workers and the elders, will see this revelation and then rise up to pray that God would give us a new revival—a revival which has never been recorded in history" (*Life-study of 1 and 2 Chronicles,* p. 15).

Day 2

(Martins)

C. If we practice living the life of a God-man, spontaneously a corporate model of a people living in the economy of God will be built up; this model will be the greatest revival in the history of the church to bring the Lord back (Phil. 1:19-21a; 3:10):

1. We need to follow the pattern of the Lord Jesus, bearing the brands of Jesus, the characteristics of His life (Gal. 6:17).

2. We need to live Christ for His magnification by the bountiful supply of the Spirit of Jesus Christ (Phil. 1:19-21a).

3. We need to be conformed to the death of Christ by the power of His resurrection (3:10).

4. "We should all declare that we want to live the life of a God-man. Eventually, the God-men will be the victors, the overcomers, the Zion within Jerusalem. This will bring in a new revival which has never been seen in history, and this will end this age" (*Life-study of 1 and 2 Chronicles,* p. 28).

Day 3

Harolds

D. We can enter into a new revival by shepherding people according to God—having the loving and forgiving heart of our Father God and the shepherding and seeking spirit of our Savior Christ (1 Pet. 5:2-3; Luke 15:20, 4; Acts 20:20):

1. We need to shepherd people according to the pattern of the Lord Jesus in His ministry for the carrying out of God's eternal economy (Matt. 9:36; John 10:11; Heb. 13:20; 1 Pet. 5:4):

   a. The content of God's entire New Testament economy in His complete salvation is Christ as the Son of Man cherishing us and as the Son of God nourishing us (Eph. 5:29).

58 % revival, GOW would be unbearable burden.
we all have desire for revival . . . —

starts our each day,
"Let Him kisses me
by kisses of Your mouth"

(SS. — 7 stages)
each stage has
begins, / course, / pulse

(draw me
our way up
to the Lord)

  b. In His heavenly ministry, Christ as the
     High Priest, with a golden girdle on His
     breast, is cherishing and nourishing the
     churches (Rev. 1:12-13).
  2. We need to shepherd people according to the
     pattern of the apostle Paul as a good shep-
     herd, taking care of God's flock (1 Tim. 1:16;
     Acts 20:28).
  3. "I hope that there will be a genuine revival
     among us by our receiving this burden of
     shepherding. If all the churches receive this
     teaching to participate in Christ's wonderful
     shepherding, there will be a big revival in the
     recovery" (*The Vital Groups,* p. 40).

Day 4 **III. The Lord's move today is through the recov-**
& *Aptos* **ery of the priesthood of the gospel in the New**
Day 5 **Testament for the organic building up of the**
     church as the Body of Christ (Rom. 15:16;
     1 Pet. 2:5, 9; Rom. 12:1; Col. 1:28-29; Matt. 16:18;
     Eph. 4:16):

His move is
(in us)

  A. We must preach the gospel by visitation (Luke 10:1-6).

(we are not
here for
a movement)

  B. We must meet in the new believers' homes, nour-
     ishing and cherishing them, so that our fruit may
     remain (Acts 5:42; John 15:16).

drawn —
↓
"rise up my love"
(call her to find Him
in this move)

  C. We must teach and perfect the saints through the
     vital group meetings unto the New Testament
     work of the ministry, unto the building up of the
     Body of Christ (Heb. 10:24-25; Eph. 4:11-12):
  1. In the vital group meetings, the believers have
     mutual fellowship and intercession, mutual
     care and shepherding, mutual teaching and
     studying of the truth, and mutual instruction
     in the pursuit of the growth in the spiritual life,
     for the promotion of the preaching of the gos-
     pel, the care for the new ones, the conducting of
     the vital group meetings, and all other kinds
     of service in the church life.

He is
skips on the hills
& leaping on mountain

(He calls us not to be
satisfied in past experience
— to join Him —

  2. The vital group meetings are the main part
     of the life and service of the church.

(she has exp. of not finding the Lord
but this is just a process of dealing — — —

(bringing testimonies to everywhere . . .)
→ He bring us to the stage to gain whole earth

D. We must lead the saints to pursue and desire after prophesying in the church meetings, speaking for the Lord, speaking forth the Lord, supplying the Lord to others, and speaking and listening to one another in mutuality for the building up of the saints and the church (1 Cor. 14:1, 3-5):

1. This kind of prophesying is what every believer can and should do (vv. 31, 24).

2. This kind of prophesying is the top point for building up the organic Body of Christ, and this will fulfill God's eternal plan according to His divine economy (vv. 1, 3, 4b, 12, 31; cf. Matt. 16:18).

3. To prohibit prophesying is a sin before God (Amos 2:12b; 7:12-17; Jer. 11:21-23).

4. In order to prophesy, we must exercise our spirit to speak with the constituting elements of prophesying—speaking what we see with the living words of this life under the inspiration of the Holy Spirit and with His enlightenment (Acts 5:20):

   a. To prophesy is to have the oracles of God (God's speaking, God's utterance, that conveys divine revelation) (1 Pet. 4:11; cf. 1 Cor. 14:24-25).

   b. When we have the human learning of the Word, the divine inspiration of the Spirit, and the clear view through the enlightening of the divine light, we will be able to prophesy (v. 31; 2:11-16).

E. The Lord desires to and will fulfill His words in Matthew 16:18, 1 Peter 2:5, Ephesians 4:11-16, and 1 Corinthians 14:26 concerning the building up of the church as a spiritual house for His dwelling, a priestly body for His service, and as the organic Body of Christ for Christ's enlargement and expression.

Day 6

Morning Nourishment

1 Tim. ...*I write* that you may know how one ought to con-
3:15 duct himself in the house of God, which is the church
       of the living God, the pillar and base of the truth.
Dan. ...But the people who know their God will show
11:32 strength and take action.
Hab. ...O Jehovah, revive Your work in the midst of the
3:2   years; in the midst of the years make *it* known; in
       wrath remember compassion.

Concerning the direction of the Lord's move today, I fully
believe that our God is living (1 Tim. 3:15; Heb. 3:12), that our
Lord is moving (Matt. 16:18), and that the Spirit is working (Rev.
5:6b). Since our God is living, our Lord is moving, and the Spirit
is working, our Triune God must still be carrying on His unique
work for the accomplishing of His eternal economy, just as He
has worked for this in the past ages and centuries. Now we need
to find out what our living, moving, and working God is doing
today on this earth. What is He carrying on today on this earth
to complete His work for His eternal economy, that is, to build up
the organic Body of His Christ? (*Elders' Training, Book 10: The
Eldership and the God-ordained Way (2)*, p. 27)

Today's Reading

Among God's elect there has always been an aspiration to be
revived. As long as you are a saved one, every day, consciously or
unconsciously, there is an aspiration with a spontaneous prayer
within you: "O Lord, revive us." Although we may not realize it,
such an aspiration has been within us through all the years of our
Christian life.

We may think that Habakkuk's prayer for revival [in 3:2] was
good for him but has nothing to do with us. However, regarding
his prayer, we need to realize that with God there is no time element. In the eyes of God, one person among His elect represents
the whole. God always considers His elect as a corporate Body.
This means that Habakkuk and we are one in the unit of God's
elect. Thus, when Habakkuk prayed for revival, we also prayed.

We prayed for revival twenty-six hundred years ago. Such a prayer is an everlasting prayer.

Many times…I charged the saints to put the God-ordained way into a living practice, but without a revival, how could we have anything living? If we endeavor to practice just the first step of the God-ordained way—to visit people for the gospel—without being revived, this will be a heavy burden that no one can bear. We…have been saved and kept on earth to do one thing—to go to disciple the nations, beginning from "Jerusalem" and spreading to "Judea," to "Samaria," and to the uttermost part of the earth (Acts 1:8). If we live for our education, a career, a good marriage, or a nice house, that is vanity of vanities. We are living…for the spreading of the Lord Jesus… to our neighborhood [and] to the entire world. If we would do this, we need to be revived. This is why the Lord has led us to practice the morning revival. (*Life-study of Malachi*, pp. 19-20)

It is a great miracle and a deep mystery that God has a way to be joined to man and mingled with man. God became man that man may become God. Such an economy is incomprehensible to both angels and man. This economy is of God's desire, and it will reach, attain, the high peak of God's goal. Ultimately the holy city, Jerusalem, will be the aggregate of all the visions and revelations throughout the Scriptures. The Triune God and the tripartite man will become a loving couple in eternity as man yet still God. Divinity and humanity will become a mutual abode, and the glory of God will be expressed in humanity radiantly in splendor to the uttermost.

I hope that the saints in all the churches throughout the earth, especially the co-workers and the elders, will see this revelation and then rise up to pray that God would give us a new revival—a revival which has never been recorded in history. (*Life-study of 1 & 2 Chronicles*, p. 15)

Further Reading: Elders' Training, Book 10: The Eldership and the God-ordained Way (2), ch. 2; Life-study of Malachi, msg. 4; The Vision of the Age, ch. 2

Enlightenment and inspiration: _____

_____

_____

_____

Morning Nourishment

Phil. According to my earnest expectation and hope that
1:20 in nothing I will be put to shame, but with all bold-
ness, as always, even now Christ will be magnified
in my body, whether through life or through death.
3:10 To know Him and the power of His resurrection
and the fellowship of His sufferings, being conformed to His death.

Since we have seen such a high peak of the divine revelation, we
need to put into practice what we have seen. Our practice will have
a success, and that success will be a new revival—the highest revival, and probably the last revival before the Lord's coming
back....We need a corporate model, a Body, a people who live the
life of a God-man. From today our practice should be to live the life
of a God-man by realizing the power of the resurrection of Christ to
take His cross as He did, to be crucified, to be conformed to His
death, every day to live another One's life (Phil. 3:10; 1:21; Gal.
2:20). Our life, our self, our flesh, our natural man, and our everything were already brought to the cross by Him. Now we are living
Him, so we should remain in His crucifixion to be conformed to the
mold of His death every moment in every part of our life. That will
cause us to spontaneously live Him as the resurrection (John
11:25). This is the living of a God-man. (*Living a Life according to
the High Peak of God's Revelation*, pp. 39-40)

Today's Reading

Our practice is not to live the life of any kind of natural man,
good or bad. Our practice is to live the life of a God-man. A God-
man is a man who is regenerated and transformed to be one with
God, taking God as his life, his person, and his everything. Eventually, this one becomes God in His life and His nature, but not in His
Godhead. This is a God-man. In the recovery today we should practice to live the life of such a God-man. This life is a life of crucifixion
by and in and with resurrection. It is a life in which I have been crucified with Christ, and it is no longer I who live but He who lives in
me (Gal. 2:20). Yet when He lives in me, He lives with me, with the

result that I live with Him (John 14:19). He lives with me, and I live with Him. We two live together in the way of mingling, a mingling of God and man.

If we live such a life, surely we will go out to contact people for the preaching of the gospel. A vital group is a group of this kind of people. The vital groups should not be practiced as a formality; they should be groups of people who live...the life of a God-man....[This] will save people, edify others, and build up the local churches even to the building up of the Body of Christ.

If we practice what we have heard, spontaneously a model will be built up. This model will be the greatest revival in the history of the church. I believe that this revival will bring the Lord back. (*Living a Life according to the High Peak of God's Revelation*, pp. 40-41)

[According to Romans 8:13] you have to put to death by the Spirit in His resurrection whatever your body does. This is to be conformed to the death of Christ by the power of His resurrection. No one in his natural life can put everything that his body does to death. But we, the God-men, who are the reproduction of the prototype, can. We can know Him and the power of His resurrection and the fellowship of His sufferings, being conformed to His death.... The Christian life is not a matter of outwardly loving people or of being meek or patient in our human ethics. We need to die every day (1 Cor. 15:31)....We need to die to live so that the many God-men can become the building material for the building up of the Body of Christ to carry out God's eternal economy. (*The Practical Way to Live a Life according to the High Peak of the Divine Revelation in the Holy Scriptures*, pp. 28-29)

We should all declare that we want to live the life of a God-man. Eventually, the God-men will be the victors, the overcomers, the Zion within Jerusalem. This will bring in a new revival which has never been seen in history, and this will end this age. (*Life-study of 1 & 2 Chronicles*, p. 28)

Further Reading: Living a Life according to the High Peak of God's Revelation, ch. 5; Life-study of 1 & 2 Chronicles, msgs. 2, 4

Enlightenment and inspiration: _____

_____

_____

_____

Morning Nourishment

1 Pet. **Shepherd the flock of God among you, overseeing**
5:2-4 **not under compulsion but willingly, according to**
God; not by seeking gain through base means but
eagerly; nor as lording it over your allotments but by
becoming patterns of the flock. And when the Chief
Shepherd is manifested, you will receive the unfad-
ing crown of glory.

We must be shepherds with the loving and forgiving heart of our Father God in His divinity and the shepherding and finding spirit of our Savior Christ in His humanity. We also must have the heavenly vision of all the divine and mystical teachings of Christ. Shepherding and teaching are the obligation of the vital groups and the basic way ordained by God to build up the Body of Christ consummating the New Jerusalem.

If [our God] had been born as a king, few would have been able to approach Him. But He was born as a poor man, and He could and did approach every class of man, especially the poor and sick ones...He became their friend. His coming in humanity made Him a very cherishing person....All people need Him to cherish them, to make them happy, comfort them, and give them rest. If He came to us in His divine status, this would intimidate us. But even the most sinful tax collectors could sit with Him as friends, eating and talking with Him (Luke 15:1; Matt. 9:10).

His ministry in the first stage of incarnation was to cherish people, to draw and attract people to Him....His death on the cross was the biggest cherishing to redeem us. Without His redemption, who could come to Him? When we heard the story of His death on the cross, our tears came down. We were attracted by Him. This is His ministry in the four Gospels. (*The Vital Groups,* pp. 55-56, 81-82).

Today's Reading

In resurrection He was transfigured to become the life-giving Spirit, the Spirit of the bountiful supply (1 Cor. 15:45b; Phil. 1:19). This Spirit is for nourishing. As the all-inclusive Spirit from Acts through the Epistles, Christ nourishes us. This nourishing produces the church, builds up the Body of Christ, and will consummate the New Jerusalem. Because of the church's degradation, Christ's nourishing becomes sevenfold intensified in the book of Revelation to bring forth the eternal goal of God, the New Jerusalem. The totality of His nourishing will be this great universal city, which is the enlargement and expression of God....The New Testament is composed of just two sections—cherishing and nourishing. With this revelation the entire New Testament has become a new book to me.

Christ is the best model of cherishing and nourishing as seen in Revelation 1[:12-13]....[These verses show] that Christ is taking care of the lampstands by being the Son of Man with a long garment. This garment is the priestly robe (Exo. 28:33-35), which shows that Christ is our great High Priest. He is also girded about at the breasts with a golden girdle. This girdle...signifies Christ's divinity becoming His energy, and the breasts signify that this golden energy is exercised and motivated by His love. His divine energy is exercised by and with His love to nourish the churches.... Christ as our High Priest takes care of the churches He has established first in His humanity to cherish the churches, to make the churches happy, pleasant, and comfortable...by dressing the lamps of the lampstand....To dress the lamps is to make them proper.

Acts 20 says that while Paul was on his way to Jerusalem, he sent word to Ephesus and called for the elders of the church. He told them that they should shepherd God's flock, which God purchased with His own blood (v. 28). The shepherding of God's flock was on Paul's heart.

I hope that there will be a genuine revival among us by our receiving this burden of shepherding. If all the churches receive this teaching to participate in Christ's wonderful shepherding, there will be a big revival in the recovery (*The Vital Groups*, pp. 82, 105-106, 61-62, 40)

Further Reading: The Vital Groups, msgs. 4, 7, 9, 11; A Word of Love to the Co-workers, Elders, Lovers, and Seekers of the Lord, ch. 2

Enlightenment and inspiration: _____

_____

_____

_____

Morning Nourishment

Rom. That I might be a minister of Christ Jesus to the Gen-
15:16 tiles, a laboring priest of the gospel of God, in order
that the offering of the Gentiles might be acceptable,
having been sanctified in the Holy Spirit.
1 Pet. You yourselves also, as living stones, are being
2:5 built up as a spiritual house into a holy priesthood
to offer up spiritual sacrifices acceptable to God
through Jesus Christ.

The Lord's recovery has been going on progressively throughout
the centuries of the history of the church, and it is still going on because it has not reached its peak yet. Throughout the centuries of
church history, the recovery has always been advancing and will continue to advance until it will reach its consummation. Even among us
in the past sixty years there have been a number of advances. In these
years, the Lord has shown us something more in His going on....
The four major items that the Lord has shown us are the priesthood
of the gospel in the New Testament, the organic building up of the
Body of Christ, the perfecting of the saints by the gifts, and the prophesying for the building up of the church as the organic Body of Christ.
These four major items are the advance of the Lord's recovery today.
(*The Advance of the Lord's Recovery Today*, pp. 7-8)

Today's Reading

[There are four] crucial points concerning the light and revelation [we have] received from the Lord...regarding the way to
meet and to serve. [First, there is] preaching the gospel and saving
people by visitation (Luke 10:1-6). [Second, there is] meeting in the
new believers' homes, nourishing and cherishing them, that our
fruit may remain (Acts 5:42; John 15:16).[Third, there is] teaching
and perfecting the saints through the small group meetings unto
the New Testament work of ministry unto the building up of the
Body of Christ (Heb. 10:24-25; Eph. 4:11-12). In the small group
meetings, the believers [have] mutual fellowship and intercession,
mutual care and shepherding, mutual teaching and studying of the
truth, and mutual instruction in the pursuit of the growth in the

spiritual life, for the promotion of the preaching of the gospel, the care for the new ones, the conducting of the small group meetings, and all other kinds of service in the church life. The small group meetings [are] the main part of the life and service of the church. [Fourth, there is] leading the saints to pursue and desire after prophesying in the church meetings, speaking for the Lord, speaking forth the Lord, supplying the Lord to others, and speaking and listening to one another in mutuality for the building up of the saints and the church (1 Cor. 14:1, 3-5). This kind of prophesying [is] what every believer can and should do (1 Cor. 14:31, 24). This kind of prophesying [is] for the building up of the church, [is] the most excelling of all gifts, and [is] highly regarded and recommended by the apostle Paul in 1 Corinthians 14 (vv. 12, 39).

Gospel preaching must be done by everyone personally through visiting others in their homes. It should not be done by calling big gospel campaigns. If there are only gospel campaigns, believers will be degraded to serve only as Levites, and only a few will then be able to serve as the exclusive priests of the gospel. The spiritual function of all the believers as priests of the gospel will be killed.

We cannot be hasty in teaching the brothers and sisters how to prophesy. You cannot teach a kindergartner to write essays. First he must go to primary school and practice writing. Furthermore, he must learn to compose sentences. Only after he has learned to compose sentence after sentence will he be able to write essays. After we gain the new ones, we must first have home meetings to nourish and cherish them. After they have grown up, then we should bring them to the small group meetings. In the small group meetings, there is the mutual teaching and learning of the truth and the pursuit of the growth in life. Whenever anyone speaks the word of God, based on the experience of life and the knowledge of the truth, the result is prophesying. (*The New Testament Priests of the Gospel*, pp. 111-112, 125, 122)

Further Reading: The Advance of the Lord's Recovery Today, chs. 1, 2, 8-10; *The New Testament Priests of the Gospel*, ch. 10

Enlightenment and inspiration: _____

_____

_____

_____

Morning Nourishment

Num. ...Oh that all Jehovah's people were prophets, that
11:29 Jehovah would put His Spirit upon them!
1 Cor. For you can all prophesy one by one that all may
14:31 learn and all may be encouraged.
    1 Pursue love, and desire earnestly spiritual *gifts*,
      but especially that you may prophesy.
    4 ...He who prophesies builds up the church.

Moses desired all of God's people to be prophets for prophesying (Num. 11:29b)....The apostle Paul taught that we all can prophesy (1 Cor. 14:31). God desires that each of the believers prophesy, that is, speak for and speak forth Him....Paul charged us not to despise prophesying (1 Thes. 5:20). Those who have rejected the Lord's ministry, the Lord's speaking, today are despising prophesying.

To prohibit prophesying is a sin before God (Amos 2:12b; 7:12-13; Jer. 11:21). Amaziah the priest charged Amos to stop speaking, to stop prophesying. Because of this, Amaziah suffered a curse.... (Amos 7:16-17). Those who stopped Jeremiah from prophesying also suffered calamity (Jer. 11:21-23). (*The Practice of the Church Life according to the God-ordained Way*, pp. 53-54)

Today's Reading

In both the Old and New Testaments, only three kinds of ministries were ordained by God—the ministries of the prophets, the priests, and the kings....In the New Testament, all of the believers are regenerated to be priests and kings (1 Pet. 2:5, 9; Rev. 1:6)...But to be a prophet depends upon our seeking.

Among the three functions of the prophet, the priest, and the king, the function of the prophet is the highest. The reason for this is that all three of these functions depend upon God's word. The kings in the Old Testament time could not receive God's word directly. The priests could receive God's word, but not directly. They received God's word indirectly through the breastplate with the Urim and the Thummim (Exo. 28:30). But the prophets, even in the Old Testament time, received God's word directly. For this reason, the prophets could reprove, instruct, and teach the kings

(2 Sam. 12:1-14), and they could also teach the priests (Hag. 2:10-19; Mal. 1:6—2:9). Because they can receive and secure the word of God directly, the prophets have the highest function.

We must gain this function [of prophesying] by our seeking. In 1 Corinthians 14:1, the word *desire* is a strong word. We must have a desire to speak for God....The most useful function for building up the church as the Body of Christ is prophesying (vv. 3-5).

According to the New Testament, there are three kinds of prophets: the prophets mentioned in Ephesians 2 and 4, the prophets mentioned in Acts 21, and the prophets mentioned in 1 Corinthians 14....The prophets mentioned in [Ephesians 2:20 and 4:11-12]...are those particularly ordained by God. The second kind of prophet is one who can predict, like Philip's daughters (Acts 21:8-9). The third kind of prophet is one who speaks for God and speaks forth God in the meetings of the church for the church's building up (1 Cor. 14:3-5).

The first kind of prophet has been ordained by God. Not all of the believers are this first kind of prophet. In speaking of this first kind of prophet, Paul said in 1 Corinthians 12:29, "Are all prophets?" Not all of the believers are prophets particularly ordained by God. However, all of the believers can be the third kind of prophet (1 Cor. 14:1, 5, 31)....Chapter 12 indicates that not all believers are prophets, but chapter 14 indicates that all believers can be prophets. This apparent contradiction is solved by the realization that there are different kinds of prophets.

Prophesying is not mainly to predict. Wuest, in his New Testament translation, renders the word *prophesies* as "imparts divine revelations to others" (1 Cor. 14:4b)....A prophet can receive and can secure the word of God directly and then speak this word for the building up of the church as the organic Body of Christ. (*The Practice of the Church Life according to the God-ordained Way,* pp. 54-57)

Further Reading: The Practice of the Church Life according to the God-ordained Way, ch. 4

Enlightenment and inspiration: _____

_____

_____

_____

angel said to Peter

Morning Nourishment

Acts Go and stand in the temple and speak to the people
5:20 all the words of this life.
1 Cor. But if all prophesy and some unbeliever or unlearned
14:24 person enters, he is convicted by all, he is examined
by all.
1 Pet. If anyone speaks, as *speaking* oracles of God...
4:11

In principle, our meetings should not be according to the worldly tradition or the natural way but should be according to the revelation of the Bible. All the members in the Body of Christ should be allowed to function. With the functioning, there is the exercise of the spirit. To exercise the spirit, we must not use man's word but should use the words in the Bible. For this reason, we need to be familiar with the words of the Bible and should soak ourselves in the Lord's word. In this way, when we open up our mouth, the Lord can be spoken forth. This is to prophesy for the Lord. I hope that when you go out to attend the home meetings, the group meetings, and the district meetings, you will strive to be free from tradition. You should not behave according to the worldly tradition or according to your natural preference. You must exercise your spirit, and you must function according to the words of the Bible. In addition, you should have the instant inspiration. In this way, you will supply and nourish others in an organic way. (*The New Testament Priests of the Gospel*, pp. 73-74)

Today's Reading

In addition to diving into the truth and pursuing after and experiencing life, you should pay special attention to these items of the organic work and should learn conscientiously. You must learn to be a New Testament priest of the gospel, going out to contact people directly, fulfilling the duty of a gospel priest, and saving sinners to offer them up to God as sacrifices. Moreover, you should continue to nourish the new believers, as a nurse would cherish her own children, that they may grow and may be led to present themselves to God as living sacrifices. After that, you still have to perfect them for the building up of the Body of Christ, until they arrive at a full-grown man. In this way, it will be easy for all of them to prophesy, and the church will be built. I hope that you will continue to get into these four items of the organic work and will act not according to the natural way but according to the organic way. (*The New Testament Priests of the Gospel,* p. 74)

[In our prophesying] we must speak with the three constituting elements of prophesying. [First,] we must possess a knowledge of the Word of God—the human element of learning (2 Tim. 3:16-17; Ezek. 3:1-4). [Second,] we must have the instant inspiration of the Holy Spirit—the divine element of inspiration (1 Cor. 14:32, 37a; 1 John 1:6-7; Rom. 8:4). [Third,] we must have a vision concerning God's interest and economy, concerning the church as the Body of Christ, concerning the local churches, concerning the world, concerning the individual saints, and even concerning ourselves—the view through the enlightening of the divine light (Eph. 1:17; 1 Cor. 2:11-12). We speak what we see with the living words of this life under the inspiration of the Holy Spirit and with His enlightenment (Acts 5:20). For the sake of the building up of the church, we need to build up a habit of speaking the word of the Lord by letting His word dwell in us richly (Col. 3:16; cf. 1 Tim. 6:20.) (*Crystallization-study Outlines—1 Corinthians,* pp. 40-41)

To prophesy is to have the oracle of God—God's speaking, God's utterance, that conveys divine revelation (1 Pet. 4:11; cf. 1 Cor. 14:24-25). When we have the human learning of the Word, the divine inspiration of the Spirit, and the clear view, we will be able to prophesy. Prophecy is always composed of the living words of this life, the inspiration of the Holy Spirit, and the clear view through the enlightening of the divine light. (*Prophesying in the Church Meetings for the Organic Building Up of the Church as the Body of Christ (Outlines),* p. 42)

Further Reading: The New Testament Priests of the Gospel, ch. 6;
  *Prophesying in the Church Meetings for the Organic Building
  Up of the Church as the Body of Christ (Outlines),* outlines 1, 6

Enlightenment and inspiration: _____

_____

_____

_____

Hymns, #864

1   Whene'er we meet with Christ endued,
      The surplus of His plenitude
    We offer unto God as food,
      And thus exhibit Christ.

         Let us exhibit Christ,
         Let us exhibit Christ;
       We'll bring His surplus to the church
         And thus exhibit Christ.

2   In Christ we live, by Christ we fight,
      On Christ we labor day and night,
    And with His surplus we unite
      To thus exhibit Christ.

3   Our life and all we are and do
      Is Christ Himself, the substance true,
    That every time we meet anew
      We may exhibit Christ.

4   In meetings Christ to God we bear
      And Christ with one another share,
    And Christ with God enjoying there,
      We thus exhibit Christ.

5   The risen Christ to God we bring,
      And Christ ascended offering,
    God's satisfaction answering,
      We thus exhibit Christ.

6   The center and reality,
      The atmosphere and ministry,
    Of all our meetings is that we
      May thus exhibit Christ.

7   The testimony and the prayer,
      And all the fellowship we share,
    The exercise of gifts, whate'er,
      Should just exhibit Christ.

8   The Father we would glorify,
      Exalting Christ the Son, thereby
    The meeting's purpose satisfy
      That we exhibit Christ.

Composition for prophecy with main point and sub-points: _____

_____
_____
_____
_____
_____
_____
_____
_____
_____
_____
_____
_____
_____
_____
_____
_____
_____
_____
_____
_____
_____
_____
_____
_____
_____
_____
_____
_____
_____
_____
_____
_____
_____
_____

The Direction of the Lord's Move Today

Scripture Reading: Eph. 4:12, 16; Rev. 19:7-9; 22:17; Dan. 2:34-35, 44-45; Rev. 11:15

Day 1

I. **The direction of the Lord's move today is to build up the organic Body of Christ as the organism of the processed and dispensing God in His Divine Trinity for His full expression (Eph. 3:19; 4:12, 16; John 15:1, 5):**

A. The highest peak in God's economy is the reality of the Body of Christ (Eph. 3:9; 4:4-6, 16):

 1. God is working Himself into us to make us the same as He is in life and nature but not in the Godhead; eventually, we will become a corporate entity—the Body of Christ—to be one with Him and to live Him for His corporate expression (Rom. 8:2, 6, 10-11, 29; Eph. 4:4-6).

 2. The reality of the Body of Christ is the corporate, Christ-magnifying, God-man living; this reality will close this age, the age of the church, and will bring Christ back for Him to take, possess, and rule over this earth in the kingdom age (Phil. 1:19-21a; 3:10-14; Gal. 2:20; Rev. 19:7-9; 20:6; Matt. 28:20b).

B. The Body of Christ is the intrinsic significance of the church; the church of God is the frame, and the Body of Christ is the organism (1 Cor. 1:2; 12:12-13, 27; Rom. 12:4-5; 16:1, 4-5).

Day 2

C. The Body of Christ is a divine constitution of the Triune God with the believers in Christ (Eph. 4:4-6):

 1. The Father, the Son, the Spirit, and man are blended and built together to become the Body of Christ.

 2. The Body of Christ is an organism, both divine and human, to express Christ (1:23).

D. The growth of the Body is the building up of the Body (4:16; Col. 2:19):

1. The growth of the Body depends on the growth
   of God, the addition of God, the increase of God,
   within us (v. 19).

2. The growth of the Body of Christ is the increase
   of Christ in the church, which results in the
   building up of the Body, by the Body itself, in
   love (Eph. 3:17a; 4:16):

   a. When Christ enters into the saints and lives
      within them, the Christ within the saints
      becomes the church (Col. 3:10-11).

   b. The Body of Christ grows by the growth of
      Christ within us and is built up this way
      (1:18; 2:19):

      (1) To grow up into Christ is to have Christ
          increase in us until we attain to a full-
          grown man (Eph. 4:13, 15).

      (2) First, we grow up into the Head; then
          we have something that is out from
          the Head for the building up of the
          Body (vv. 15-16).

   c. The love in which the Body builds itself up
      is not our own love but the love of God in
      Christ, which becomes the love of Christ
      in us, by which we love Christ and the fel-
      low members of His Body (1 John 4:7-8, 11,
      16, 19; Rom. 5:5; 8:39).

Day 3

II. **The direction of the Lord's move today is to
prepare the bride as the counterpart of the
Bridegroom for the eternal marriage of the redeeming God with His redeemed (Rev. 19:7-8;
22:17; 21:1-2, 9-10):**

   A. The marriage of the Lamb is the issue of the com-
      pletion of God's New Testament economy, which is
      to obtain for Christ a bride, the church, through
      His judicial redemption and by His organic salva-
      tion in the divine life (Gen. 2:22; Rom. 5:10; Rev.
      19:7-9; 21:2, 9-11).

   B. The church as the bride of Christ is a matter of sat-
      isfaction and rest in love (Gen. 2:21-23; Zeph. 3:17).

C. The Lord's recovery is for the preparation of the
   bride of Christ, who is composed of all His overcomers (Rev. 19:7-9):
   1. All the overcomers will be the New Jerusa-
      lem as the bride of Christ for one thousand
      years in its initial and fresh stage (v. 7).
   2. Eventually, all of the believers will join the over-
      comers to consummate and complete the New
      Jerusalem in full as the wife of Christ in the
      new heaven and new earth for eternity (21:2, 9-10).
D. The readiness of the corporate bride depends
   on the maturity in life of the overcomers (19:7;
   Heb. 6:1; Phil. 3:12-15; Eph. 4:13):
   1. In the New Testament the word *mature* is
      used to refer to the believers' being full-grown
      and perfected in the life of God, indicating
      that we need to grow and mature unto perfec-
      tion in the divine life (Matt. 5:48).

Day 4

korean

   2. We need to continue to grow until we are
      matured in the divine life to become a full-
      grown man, at the measure of the stature of
      the fullness of Christ (Eph. 4:13).
E. The overcomers are not separate individuals but
   a corporate bride; for this, building is needed
   (Matt. 16:18; Eph. 2:21-22; 4:15-16):
   1. The overcomers are not only mature in life
      but are also built together as one bride (Rev.
      19:7-9; 21:2, 9-11).
   2. The central and divine thought of the Bible is
      that God is seeking a building as the mingling of
      Himself with humanity for His eternal, corpo-
      rate expression (Gen. 2:22-23; Rev. 21:2, 9-11).
F. As the bride, the church needs beauty (Eph. 5:27;
   S. S. 4:7-15):
   1. The beauty of the bride is for the presentation
      of the bride to the Bridegroom (Eph. 5:27).
   2. The beauty of the bride comes from the Christ
      who is wrought into the church and who is
      then expressed through the church (3:17a).

Day 5

III. **The direction of the Lord's move today is to bring in the kingdom of God as the spreading of the divine life for God's eternal administration in the fulfillment of His eternal economy (Luke 19:12, 15a; Dan. 2:34-35, 44-45; Rev. 11:15):**

A. The kingdom of God is Christ Himself as the seed of life sown into us, growing in us, spreading in us, and maturing in us until there is a full harvest—the manifestation of the kingdom (Mark 4:26-29; Matt. 13:43):

1. The kingdom of God is actually the God-man, the Lord Jesus, sown as a seed into the believers and developing into a realm over which God can rule as His kingdom in His divine life (Luke 17:20-21; Mark 4:3, 26-29):

a. The Lord Jesus, who is the embodiment of the Triune God, came to be the kingdom of God by sowing Himself as the seed of the kingdom into God's chosen people (Col. 2:9; Luke 17:20-21; Matt. 13:3-23).

b. Christ establishes the kingdom by sowing Himself as the seed of life into believing people so that the kingdom may grow; this is absolutely a matter of the growth in life, not of our work (1 Pet. 1:23; 1 John 3:9; Matt. 13:3).

c. Regeneration is the entrance into the kingdom of God, and the growth of the divine life within the believers is the development of the kingdom of God (John 3:3, 5; 2 Pet. 1:3-11; Dan. 2:35, 44; Rev. 11:15).

2. After this seed has been sown into the believers, it will grow and develop within them into the kingdom of God, which is for the fulfillment of God's eternal purpose and also for their blessing and enjoyment (Col. 1:13).

Day 6

B. The increase of the stone into a great mountain signifies the increase of Christ in His administration to be the kingdom of God; the church is

Christ's increase in life, but the eternal kingdom of God is Christ's increase in administration; hence, Christ is not only the church but also the kingdom (Dan. 2:35, 44; John 3:29-30; 1 Cor. 12:12; Mark 4:26-29; Luke 17:21).

C. The coming of Christ will be the opening of the eternal kingdom of God; hence, Christ's coming will be the landmark that closes human government and brings in the eternal kingdom of God (Rev. 11:15):

1. In God's economy, Christ, by His upcoming appearing, will smash and crush the aggregate of human government and establish the eternal kingdom of God (Dan. 2:34-35).

2. The great human image will be replaced with a great mountain, signifying the eternal kingdom of God, which will fill the whole earth; this means that after Christ comes to crush the aggregate of human government, He will usher in the eternal kingdom of God on earth (vv. 44-45).

3. The goal of the divine history within the human history is to have the corporate Christ—Christ with His overcomers—as the crushing stone to be His dispensational instrument to end this age and become a great mountain, the kingdom of God (vv. 28, 31-45; Rev. 12:1-2, 5, 10-11; 14:1-5; 19:7-21).

4. During the church age, Christ is building up the church, the Body, to be His bride, and He will return with His overcoming bride as the smiting stone to crush the aggregate of human government and usher in the age of God's dominion over the entire earth (Matt. 16:18; Dan. 2:34-35, 44-45; Rev. 11:15-17).

Morning Nourishment

Phil   To know Him and the power of His resurrection
3:10   and the fellowship of His sufferings, being con-
      formed to His death.

Eph.   Out from whom all the Body, being joined together
4:16   and being knit together through every joint of the
      rich supply and *through* the operation in the meas-
      ure of each one part, causes the growth of the Body
      unto the building up of itself in love.

The Lord's move today has a direction....The direction of the
Lord's move today is, first, to build up His organic Body (Eph. 4:12),
a Body full of Himself and built up with Himself (Col. 3:11) as the
life-giving Spirit, who is the essence, the element, and the reality of
the church as the organic Body of Christ (Eph. 4:4a). Such a Body
becomes the organism of the processed Triune God (John 15:1, 5,
8a), who is dispensing Himself in His divine Trinity (2 Cor. 13:14) to
saturate the Body of Christ organically that it might be His full expression in the universe (Eph. 3:19). (*Elders' Training, Book 10: The
Eldership and the God-ordained Way (2)*, p. 30)

Today's Reading

The highest peak in God's economy [is] the reality of the Body of
Christ. We know the term *the Body of Christ*. We may even have
seen the revelation of the Body of Christ. Yet we have to admit that
thus far, over the past seventy-two years, through such a long time,
we can see very little of the reality of the Body of Christ within us
and among us. I am speaking not of the revelation, not even of the
vision, but of the reality of the Body of Christ. This reality has nothing to do with any kind of organization or with anything which
remains in the nature of organization. Also, the reality of the Body
of Christ is not a system in any way, because no system is organic.
The reality of the Body of Christ is absolutely and altogether organic. (*The Practical Points concerning Blending*, p. 30)

God's aim in His economy is to have a group of human beings
who have His life and nature inwardly and His image and likeness
outwardly. This group of people is a corporate entity, the Body of

Christ, to be one with Him and live Him for His corporate expression. As God is expressed not only by the Body but also through the Body, He is glorified. When He is glorified, His people are also glorified in His glorification. In this way God and man are one in glory....Nevertheless, no matter how much we are one with God, we do not share His Godhead and will never share it. Man remains man, and God remains God. (*Life-study of Jeremiah*, p. 82)

Just to be one who is according to God's heart, like David, and just to be partly right and good in the eyes of God, like some honest Christians, do not qualify us to partake of Christ in full and to enjoy all the rights in Him that we may become adequately the church as the Body of Christ and as the kingdom of God and of Christ. Conformity to Christ's death by the power of His resurrection is required of us, the New Testament overcomers, that we may die to ourselves, our natural man, and live to God in resurrection. A life of living Christ, magnifying Christ, and moving and acting with Christ by the bountiful supply of the all-inclusive, life-giving Spirit, doing everything in and according to the Spirit, is indispensable for us, God's New Testament seekers, to be winners in the racecourse of the divine life that we may fully enjoy Christ as the God-given good land in the church age and be gloriously rewarded to partake of Christ, in the fullest sense, in the kingdom age. (*Life-study of 1 & 2 Kings*, pp. 157-158)

The Body is the intrinsic significance of the church. If there were no Body, the church would have no meaning. The church makes no sense without the Body. But hallelujah, there is the Body! Without the Body, the church makes no sense, but with the Body, there is the intrinsic significance of the church....What is the difference between the church and the Body? We need to see that the church of God is the frame and the Body of Christ is the organism. (*The Issue of the Divine Dispensing of the Processed Trinity and the Transmitting of the Transcending Christ*, p. 91)

Further Reading: The Practical Points concerning Blending, chs. 4-5; *Life-study of Jeremiah*, msg. 12

Enlightenment and inspiration: _____

_____

_____

_____

WEEK 6 — DAY 2

Eph 4:15   grow up into Christ
4:16 ⎯ out of Christ, *at the Body*
growth, builds

100

Morning Nourishment

Eph. But holding to truth in love, we may grow up into
4:15 Him in all things, who is the Head, Christ.
Col. And not holding the Head, out from whom all the
2:19 Body, being richly supplied and knit together by
means of the joints and sinews, grows with the
growth of God.

The Body of Christ is the divine constitution of the Triune
God with the believers in Christ. Ephesians 4:4-6 shows us the
constitution of the three divine persons with all His chosen people. So we have the one Body, one Spirit, one Lord, and one God
and Father mingled together....The Body of Christ is a mingling
of the Divine Trinity with all His chosen human beings. It is a
mingling of divinity with humanity....The Body of Christ is an
organism. On the one hand, it is divine. On the other hand, it is
human to express the divine and human Christ, who is both the
complete God and the perfect man. (*The Issue of the Divine Dispensing of the Processed Trinity and the Transmitting of the
Transcending Christ*, pp. 92-93)

Today's Reading

The growth of the Body depends on what comes out of Christ
as the Head. If we do not receive the supply that comes from
Christ as the Head, the Body cannot grow. But when the Body is
supplied by holding the Head, the Body grows with the growth of
God. The Body grows out from the Head, for all the supply comes
from the Head. (*The Conclusion of the New Testament*, p. 2267)

When we say that the church is organic, we do not mean that it
is an organism composed of our natural life. Rather, it is an organism composed of the life in our spirit, which is Christ Himself. The
resurrected Christ is the life-giving Spirit. This Spirit enters into
us who have received Him. Hence, within us we have the same life
and the same spirit. In this one life we become organic, being joined
together as one. The problem now is that we have two lives within
us. One is the original natural life; the other is the Lord Jesus as
our life. Which life are we living by? If we live by our natural life, we

are not the church. If we live according to Christ and live Christ, we are the church. The church is Christ Himself in all of us. When Christ is in Himself, He is just Christ. When He enters into the saints and lives with the saints, the Christ within the saints becomes the church. The reality of the church is Christ living in us. The key to the building up of the Body of Christ is to live Christ. If we live our natural life, the Body of Christ will not be built up. For this reason we must deny and reject our natural life and must put the natural life aside. In this way, Christ will have the proper place within us and will be able to increase day by day. This is the building up of the Body of Christ. The Body of Christ grows by the growth of Christ within us and is built up this way. (*The Economy of God and the Building Up of the Body of Christ,* pp. 66-67)

The word "Head" in Ephesians 4:15 indicates that our growth in life with Christ should be the growth of the members in the Body under the Head. This means that our growth must be in the Body. In order to grow into the Head, we must surely be in the Body.

In verse 16 Paul continues, "Out from whom all the Body, being joined together and being knit together through every joint of the rich supply, and through the operation in the measure of each one part, causes the growth of the Body unto the building up of itself in love." Our growth in life is to grow into the Head, Christ, but our function in the Body is to function out from Him. First, we grow up into the Head. Then we have something which is out from the Head. (*The Conclusion of the New Testament,* p. 2492)

[The love in Ephesians 4:15] is not our own love but the love of God in Christ, which becomes the love of Christ in us, by which we love Christ and the fellow members of His Body. It is in such a love that we hold to truth, that is, to Christ with His Body, and are kept from being influenced by the winds of teaching and from bringing in elements that are foreign to the Body. (Eph. 4:15, footnote 2)

Further Reading: The Issue of the Divine Dispensing of the Processed Trinity and the Transmitting of the Transcending Christ, chs. 6-7; The Economy of God and the Building Up of the Body of Christ, ch. 6

Enlightenment and inspiration: _____

_____

_____

_____

Morning Nourishment

Rev. Let us rejoice and exult, and let us give the glory to
19:7 Him, for the marriage of the Lamb has come, and
His wife has made herself ready.
21:9 ...Come here; I will show you the bride, the wife of
the Lamb.

The direction of the Lord's move today is, second, to prepare
His bride, the church, as His (the Bridegroom's) counterpart
(John 3:29-30) for the eternal marriage (Rev. 19:7-8), the universal marriage, of the redeeming God with His redeemed people
(Rev. 22:17; 21:1-2, 9b-10). This universal marriage was typified
by the union of the people of Israel with their redeeming God
(Isa. 54:5; Hosea 2:19) and is clearly revealed in the New Testament (Eph. 5:25-27, 32). (*Elders' Training, Book 10: The Eldership and the God-ordained Way (2),* p. 30)

Today's Reading

The marriage of the Lamb is the issue of the completion of God's
New Testament economy. God's economy...is to obtain for Christ a
bride, the church, through His redemption and divine life. By the
continual working of the Holy Spirit through all the centuries, this
goal will be attained at the end of this age. Then the bride, consist-
ing of the overcoming believers, will be ready.

The church as the counterpart of Christ implies satisfaction
and rest in love....If we say that we are the church, then we must
ask if Christ has His rest among us. This is a serious matter. A
group of Christians should not be so quick to claim that they are
the church. To be the church is to render to Christ the adequate
satisfaction and rest in love. Christ needs such a counterpart. The
church is not merely a gathering of God's called ones. The church,
as Christ's counterpart, is a satisfaction and rest to Christ in love.

God's intention is that the church will consummate in the
New Jerusalem. All the regenerated and perfected believers as
members of the church, represented by the twelve apostles (Rev.
21:14), will be the components of the New Jerusalem. After
the dispensation of grace, there will be the dispensation of the

kingdom. During this dispensation, all the perfected ones, including the overcomers of the Old Testament and the overcomers of the New Testament, will be the totality of overcomers to be the New Jerusalem. They will be the New Jerusalem in its first stage, the stage of the millennium. During this stage, the New Jerusalem will be Christ's bride. (*The Conclusion of the New Testament*, pp. 2424, 2276, 2542)

What God wants is the New Jerusalem, which will be the totality of what the overcomers are. Eventually, all the overcomers will be the New Jerusalem, as the bride of Christ for one thousand years, in its initial and fresh stage. These one thousand years will be counted as one day (2 Pet. 3:8), the wedding day. This will be the initial and fresh stage of the New Jerusalem as the bride of Christ.

Eventually, all of the believers will join the overcomers to make the New Jerusalem larger than it was in the thousand-year kingdom. That will consummate and complete the New Jerusalem in full, as the tabernacle of God and the wife of Christ in the new heaven and new earth for eternity. (*The Overcomers*, pp. 104-105)

According to Revelation 19:8 and 9, the wife, the bride of Christ, in verse 7 consists only of the overcoming believers during the millennium, whereas the bride, the wife, in Revelation 21:2 is composed of all the saved saints after the millennium for eternity. The readiness of the bride in 19:7 depends on the maturity in life of the overcomers. (*The Conclusion of the New Testament*, pp. 2424-2425)

The meaning of the word *mature* in Greek is "at the end point." When...used to describe organisms, it denotes completion, full growth, and maturity. This word is used many times in the New Testament, referring to the believers' being full-grown, mature, and perfected in the life of God, which they receive at the time of regeneration. It indicates that although we receive the life of God when we are regenerated, after regeneration we still need to grow and mature unto perfection in this life. (*Life Lessons*, vol. 4, p. 69)

Further Reading: The Overcomers, ch. 6; The Conclusion of the New Testament, msgs. 226-229

Enlightenment and inspiration: _____

_____

_____

_____

(oldness)

Morning Nourishment

Eph. **That He might present the church to Himself glori-**
5:27 **ous, not having spot or wrinkle or any such things,**
but that she would be holy and without blemish.
Rev. **And I saw the holy city, New Jerusalem, coming**
21:2 **down out of heaven from God, prepared as a bride**
adorned for her husband.

Paul's concept in Ephesians 4 is absolutely different from the concept in today's Christianity. The basic concept in this chapter is that of growth until we all arrive at a full-grown man. As all mothers know, growth of children comes by feeding, not mainly by teaching. When we all arrive at a full-grown man, we shall no longer be children spiritually. On the human side the main need is not doctrine; it is growth. We need to grow until we arrive at a full-grown man.

In verse 15…Paul does not say that we shall grow up into the knowledge of Bible doctrine. On the contrary, he says that we shall grow up into Christ as the Head. This indicates that what is needed on the human side for the fulfillment of God's economy is growth. (*Life-study of Ephesians*, pp. 747-748)

Today's Reading

As the Lamb, Christ needs a wedding. The Gospel of John reveals that Christ is the Lamb who came to take away sin (1:29) and also the Bridegroom who came that He might have the bride. Christ's goal is not to remove sin; His goal is to have the bride. In the book of Revelation we see that Christ is the Lamb and the coming Bridegroom. As the Bridegroom, He must have a wedding.

Revelation 19:7b says, "His wife has made herself ready." The readiness of the bride depends on the maturity in life of the overcomers. Furthermore, the overcomers are not separate individuals but a corporate bride. For this, building is needed. The overcomers are not only mature in life but are also built together as one bride. (*The Conclusion of the New Testament*, p. 2278)

We do believe that there is a paradise prepared by God, but we must realize and remember well that the divine thought in the entire Scriptures is not that God is seeking a physical habitation. A physical habitation can never satisfy God. The central and divine thought of the Scriptures is that God is seeking a divine building as the mingling of Himself with humanity. He is seeking a living composition of living persons redeemed by and mingled with Himself.

After His creation, God began and is still carrying out the work of the divine building. Even today God is doing the work of the divine building, which is to mingle Himself with man. We preach the gospel not merely to win souls or save souls from hell but to minister God Himself through the Spirit to man so that God can be mingled with man. In this way we gain the materials for the divine building. Likewise, we minister Christ to the saints so that they can be mingled and built up together with Christ. This is the basic and central thought behind what we do. (*The Building of God,* p. 13)

In [Ephesians 5] we come to the presentation of the church to Christ. At the time of this presentation, the church will be the bride, not the new man. As the new man, the church needs the functions. But as the bride, the church needs beauty. The growth in chapter 4 is for the function of the new man, whereas the beauty in chapter 5 is for the presentation of the bride.

Christ is now preparing us to be His bride. The time is coming when He will present the bride to Himself. Surely at the time of her presentation to Christ, the bride will not have any wrinkles or spots. In His bride Christ will behold nothing but beauty. This beauty will be the reflection of what He is. Do you know where the beauty of the bride comes from? It comes from the very Christ who is wrought into the church and who is then expressed through the church. Our beauty is not our behavior. Our only beauty is the reflection of Christ, the shining out of Christ from within us. What Christ appreciates in us is the expression of Himself in us. Nothing less than this will meet His standard or win His appreciation. (*Life-study of Ephesians,* pp. 798, 800)

Further Reading: Life-study of Ephesians, msgs. 89, 95; *The Building of God,* ch. 1

Enlightenment and inspiration: _____

_____

_____

_____

Morning Nourishment

1 Pet. **Having been regenerated not of corruptible seed**
1:23 **but of incorruptible, through *the* living and abiding**
word of God.

2 Pet. **For in this way the entrance into the eternal kingdom**
1:11 **of our Lord and Savior Jesus Christ will be richly *and***
bountifully supplied to you.

The direction of the Lord's move today is, third, to bring in the kingdom of God as the spreading of the divine life, which is Christ. The kingdom of God is actually Christ Himself as the seed of life sown into His believers in the church age (Luke 17:21; Mark 4:3, 8, 26) and spreading in His increasing (John 3:30) to be the enlarged, upcoming kingdom of God, which He will bring in at His coming back (Luke 19:12, 15a; Rev. 11:15). This is signified by the stone (Christ) that became a great mountain (the kingdom in the millennium), as revealed in Daniel 2:34-35. This upcoming, enlarged kingdom of God will be God's universal government in the new heaven and new earth for God's eternal administration in the fulfillment of God's eternal economy in Christ as God's ultimately consummated household administration in eternity.

Both God and Christ are aspiring to see the Body of Christ built up, to see the bride prepared, and to see the kingdom brought in, that Christ may have a Body, that Christ may have His bride, and that God may have a kingdom on this earth for His eternal economy. (*Elders' Training, Book 10: The Eldership and the God-ordained Way (2)*, pp. 30-31)

Today's Reading

The kingdom of God is the Lord Jesus as the seed of life sown into His believers, God's chosen people, and developing into a realm which God may rule as His kingdom in His divine life. Its entrance is regeneration (John 3:5), and its development is the believers' growth in the divine life (2 Pet. 1:3-11). It is the church today, in which the faithful believers live (Rom. 14:17), and it will develop into the coming kingdom as an inheritance reward (Gal. 5:21; Eph. 5:5) to the overcoming saints in the millennium (Rev.

20:4, 6). Eventually, it will consummate in the New Jerusalem as the eternal kingdom of God, an eternal realm of the eternal blessing of God's eternal life for all God's redeemed to enjoy in the new heaven and new earth for eternity (Rev. 21:1-4; 22:1-5). (*The Conclusion of the New Testament,* p. 2640)

The kingdom is Christ Himself as the seed of life sown into us, growing in us, spreading in us, and maturing in us until there is a full harvest. The full harvest is the manifestation of the kingdom.

In the first chapter of the New Testament we have the record of a wonderful One, Christ, who is recommended to us as the seed of the kingdom. We need a deeper understanding concerning this seed of the kingdom. (*The Kingdom,* p. 37)

In the New Testament the kingdom of God is not a material realm in which God exercises His authority to carry out His governmental administration so that we may enter this realm to enjoy an eternal blessing....What is revealed in the New Testament regarding the kingdom of God is that the kingdom is a person, not a material realm. This Person, the Lord Jesus Christ, the Son of God, is the embodiment of the Triune God. This One who is the embodiment of the Triune God came to be the kingdom. In Mark 4 He says that the kingdom is like a sower sowing the seed. Both the Sower and the seed are the Lord Himself. The Lord Jesus came to sow Himself as the seed of the kingdom into God's chosen people. In His ministry He did not sow anything other than Himself as the seed of the kingdom. (*Life-study of Mark,* p. 553)

Christ establishes the kingdom of the heavens not by fighting or teaching, but by sowing Himself as the seed of life into believing people so that the kingdom of the heavens may grow up. The establishment of the kingdom of the heavens is absolutely a matter of growth in life. To establish the kingdom is to grow the kingdom. The kingdom is not established by outward working, but by inward growing. (*Life-study of Matthew,* p. 438)

Further Reading: The Conclusion of the New Testament, msg. 250; *Life-study of Mark,* msgs. 64-65

Enlightenment and inspiration: _____

_____

_____

_____

Morning Nourishment

Dan. ...And the stone that struck the image became a
2:35 great mountain and filled the whole earth.
44 And in the days of those kings the God of the heavens will raise up a kingdom which will never be
destroyed...; it will crush and put an end to all
these kingdoms; and it will stand forever.

The great mountain [in Daniel 2:35] signifies the eternal kingdom of God, which will fill the whole earth forever (v. 44; 7:13-14)....
The increase of the stone into a great mountain signifies the
increase of Christ (cf. John 3:29-30). The church is Christ's increase
in life, but the eternal kingdom of God is Christ's increase in administration (Mark 4:26-29). Hence, Christ is not only the church
but also the kingdom of God (1 Cor. 12:12; Luke 17:21). As the
stone, Christ is the centrality of God's move, and as the mountain,
He is the universality. Hence, He is the all-inclusive One, the One
who fills all in all (Eph. 1:23). (Dan. 2:35, footnote 3)

Today's Reading

The coming of Christ will also be the opening of the eternal
kingdom of God. Hence, Christ's coming will be the landmark
which closes human government and brings in the eternal kingdom of God.

In God's economy, Christ has terminated the old creation for the
germination of the new creation in His resurrection through His
death. This was achieved in His first coming. In God's economy,
Christ, by His upcoming appearing, will also smash and crush the
aggregate of human government throughout the history of mankind
and will establish the eternal kingdom of God....The entire world
situation is under the rule of the heavens by the God of the heavens, to match His economy for Christ. Today the world situation,
especially in Europe and the countries around the Mediterranean
Sea, has been balanced and brought into a condition which is ready
for Christ's return. He is at the door and the time is near. As we see
this situation, we must wake up and realize that the world is not
for us. We are for Christ, and every day we must prepare ourselves

to meet Him. Then we will receive a reward from Him.

This increase of the stone into a great mountain signifies the increase of Christ. The fact that Christ can increase is clearly revealed in John 3. Referring to Christ, verse 30 says, "He must increase." The increase in this verse is the bride spoken of in verse 29: "He who has the bride is the bridegroom." Christ, therefore, has an increase, and this increase is His bride. Just as Eve was the increase of Adam, the bride is the increase of Christ as the Bridegroom....In life Christ increases to become the church; in administration Christ increases to become the eternal kingdom of God....Both the church and the kingdom are His increase.

After crushing the human government, God will have cleared up the entire universe. The old creation will be gone, and the human government will become chaff blown away by the wind. Then the corporate Christ, Christ with His overcomers, will become a great mountain to fill the whole earth, making the whole earth God's kingdom (Dan. 2:35, 44). Both the earth and the heaven will then be new for God to exercise His kingdom.

When Christ comes as the smiting stone, He will not come alone. Rather, He will come with His bride. By that time Christ will have already gained the church, and He will have married His bride, as described in Revelation 19. After His wedding He will come both as the smiting stone and as the One who will tread the winepress (Rev. 19:15; 14:19-20; Isa. 63:2-3).

The parable of the seed in Mark 4:26-29 reveals how the kingdom of God is the increase of Christ. Verse 26 says, "So is the kingdom of God: as if a man cast seed on the earth." This seed is Christ as the embodiment of the divine life....This seed sprouts, grows, bears fruit, matures, and brings forth a harvest (vv. 27-28). From the time Christ came to sow Himself into the "soil" of humanity, He has been growing and increasing. Eventually, this increase will become the great mountain that fills the whole earth to be the eternal kingdom of God. (*Life-study of Daniel*, pp. 2, 5, 18, 75, 17, 18)

Further Reading: Life-study of Daniel, msgs. 1, 3, 12

Enlightenment and inspiration: _____

_____

_____

_____

Hymns, #1101

1 Lo, the kingdom of the world is now
    the kingdom of the Lord!
O what joy to all the saints does
    His eternal reign afford!
Let us swell the mighty chorus of His
    praise in one accord —
      The victory is won!

    Vict'ry, vict'ry, Hallelujah!
    Vict'ry, vict'ry, Hallelujah!
    Vict'ry, vict'ry, Hallelujah!
      The victory is won!

2 That great dragon, the old serpent
    called the devil, down is cast;
Satan and his fallen angels' long deceiving
    days are past!
Now our praises like a thunder through the
    universe shall blast —
      The victory is won!

3 Now is come salvation, power, and the
    kingdom of our God;
The accuser of the brethren underneath
    our feet is trod!
The authority of Christ is now the church's
    ruling rod —
      The victory is won!

4 By the Lamb's redeeming blood th' accuser
    we have overcome;
By our word of testimony, all declaring,
    "It is done!"
Unto death, our souls not loving — all the
    glory to the Son!
      The victory is won!

5   Oh, but brothers, sisters, listen to another
       mighty voice,
    "Babylon is fallen, fallen"—what a reason
       to rejoice!
    O how blest that coming out from her was
       our eternal choice —
          The victory is won!

6   She's the mother of the harlots, Myst'ry,
       Babylon the Great!
    O how all her evil fornication we have learned
       to hate!
    But our God has doubly judged her — this our
       spirits doth elate.
          The victory is won!

7   Hallelujah! Glory, power to the Lord our
       God belong!
    True and righteous are His judgments on
       the harlot for her wrong!
    See, her smoke is rising! Echo hallelujah
       in your song —
          The victory is won!

8   "Praise our God now, all ye servants, small
       and great," His voice constrains.
    As the sound of many waters, we will thunder
       our refrains:
    Hallelujah, hallelujah, for the Lord Almighty
       reigns!
          The victory is won!

9   Now rejoice and be exceeding glad! What
       glory is displayed!
    For the marriage of the Lamb, the wife all
       ready now is made!
    In fine linen, bright and pure, 'twas granted
       her to be arrayed —
          The victory is won!

continued

10 Now the devil's in the lake of fire, for John
    has seen him there;
Hallelujah, never more need we his
    provocations bear!
What a triumph for the saints his judgment
    boldly to declare —
      The victory is won!

11 Now behold the greatest wonder—New
    Jerusalem descend!
She's the building of the Triune God with
    man—a perfect blend!
She's the Bride, prepared, adorned for Christ —
    of all God's work, the end!
      The victory is won!

12 It's the tabernacle of our God, His dwelling
    place with men;
In His holiness and glory He's expressed
    through all of them.
"It is done!" O brothers, see it! See the
    New Jerusalem!
      The victory is won!

    Hallelujah, hallelujah!
    Hallelujah, hallelujah!
    Hallelujah, hallelujah!
      The victory is won!

Composition for prophecy with main point and sub-points: _____

_____

_____

_____

_____

_____

_____

_____

_____

_____

_____

_____

_____

_____

_____

_____

_____

_____

_____

_____

_____

_____

_____

_____

_____

_____

_____

_____

_____

_____

_____

_____

_____

_____

_____

_____

_____

Reading Schedule for the Recovery Version of the Old Testament with Footnotes

Wk.	Lord's Day	Monday	Tuesday	Wednesday	Thursday	Friday	Saturday
1	☐ Gen 1:1-5	☐ 1:6-23	☐ 1:24-31	☐ 2:1-9	☐ 2:10-25	☐ 3:1-13	☐ 3:14-24
2	☐ 4:1-26	☐ 5:1-32	☐ 6:1-22	☐ 7:1—8:3	☐ 8:4-22	☐ 9:1-29	☐ 10:1-32
3	☐ 11:1-32	☐ 12:1-20	☐ 13:1-18	☐ 14:1-24	☐ 15:1-21	☐ 16:1-16	☐ 17:1-27
4	☐ 18:1-33	☐ 19:1-38	☐ 20:1-18	☐ 21:1-34	☐ 22:1-24	☐ 23:1—24:27	☐ 24:28-67
5	☐ 25:1-34	☐ 26:1-35	☐ 27:1-46	☐ 28:1-22	☐ 29:1-35	☐ 30:1-43	☐ 31:1-55
6	☐ 32:1-32	☐ 33:1—34:31	☐ 35:1-29	☐ 36:1-43	☐ 37:1-36	☐ 38:1—39:23	☐ 40:1—41:13
7	☐ 41:14-57	☐ 42:1-38	☐ 43:1-34	☐ 44:1-34	☐ 45:1-28	☐ 46:1-34	☐ 47:1-31
8	☐ 48:1-22	☐ 49:1-15	☐ 49:16-33	☐ 50:1-26	☐ Exo 1:1-22	☐ 2:1-25	☐ 3:1-22
9	☐ 4:1-31	☐ 5:1-23	☐ 6:1-30	☐ 7:1-25	☐ 8:1-32	☐ 9:1-35	☐ 10:1-29
10	☐ 11:1-10	☐ 12:1-14	☐ 12:15-36	☐ 12:37-51	☐ 13:1-22	☐ 14:1-31	☐ 15:1-27
11	☐ 16:1-36	☐ 17:1-16	☐ 18:1-27	☐ 19:1-25	☐ 20:1-26	☐ 21:1-36	☐ 22:1-31
12	☐ 23:1-33	☐ 24:1-18	☐ 25:1-22	☐ 25:23-40	☐ 26:1-14	☐ 26:15-37	☐ 27:1-21
13	☐ 28:1-21	☐ 28:22-43	☐ 29:1-21	☐ 29:22-46	☐ 30:1-10	☐ 30:11-38	☐ 31:1-17
14	☐ 31:18—32:35	☐ 33:1-23	☐ 34:1-35	☐ 35:1-35	☐ 36:1-38	☐ 37:1-29	☐ 38:1-31
15	☐ 39:1-43	☐ 40:1-38	☐ Lev 1:1-17	☐ 2:1-16	☐ 3:1-17	☐ 4:1-35	☐ 5:1-19
16	☐ 6:1-30	☐ 7:1-38	☐ 8:1-36	☐ 9:1-24	☐ 10:1-20	☐ 11:1-47	☐ 12:1-8
17	☐ 13:1-28	☐ 13:29-59	☐ 14:1-18	☐ 14:19-32	☐ 14:33-57	☐ 15:1-33	☐ 16:1-17
18	☐ 16:18-34	☐ 17:1-16	☐ 18:1-30	☐ 19:1-37	☐ 20:1-27	☐ 21:1-24	☐ 22:1-33
19	☐ 23:1-22	☐ 23:23-44	☐ 24:1-23	☐ 25:1-23	☐ 25:24-55	☐ 26:1-24	☐ 26:25-46
20	☐ 27:1-34	☐ Num 1:1-54	☐ 2:1-34	☐ 3:1-51	☐ 4:1-49	☐ 5:1-31	☐ 6:1-27
21	☐ 7:1-41	☐ 7:42-88	☐ 7:89—8:26	☐ 9:1-23	☐ 10:1-36	☐ 11:1-35	☐ 12:1—13:33
22	☐ 14:1-45	☐ 15:1-41	☐ 16:1-50	☐ 17:1—18:7	☐ 18:8-32	☐ 19:1-22	☐ 20:1-29
23	☐ 21:1-35	☐ 22:1-41	☐ 23:1-30	☐ 24:1-25	☐ 25:1-18	☐ 26:1-65	☐ 27:1-23
24	☐ 28:1-31	☐ 29:1-40	☐ 30:1—31:24	☐ 31:25-54	☐ 32:1-42	☐ 33:1-56	☐ 34:1-29
25	☐ 35:1-34	☐ 36:1-13	☐ Deut 1:1-46	☐ 2:1-37	☐ 3:1-29	☐ 4:1-49	☐ 5:1-33
26	☐ 6:1—7:26	☐ 8:1-20	☐ 9:1-29	☐ 10:1-22	☐ 11:1-32	☐ 12:1-32	☐ 13:1—14:21

Reading Schedule for the Recovery Version of the Old Testament with Footnotes

Wk.	Lord's Day	Monday	Tuesday	Wednesday	Thursday	Friday	Saturday
27	☐ 14:22—15:23	☐ 16:1-22	☐ 17:1—18:8	☐ 18:9—19:21	☐ 20:1—21:17	☐ 21:18—22:30	☐ 23:1-25
28	☐ 24:1-22	☐ 25:1-19	☐ 26:1-19	☐ 27:1-26	☐ 28:1-68	☐ 29:1-29	☐ 30:1—31:29
29	☐ 31:30—32:52	☐ 33:1-29	☐ 34:1-12	☐ Josh 1:1-18	☐ 2:1-24	☐ 3:1-17	☐ 4:1-24
30	☐ 5:1-15	☐ 6:1-27	☐ 7:1-26	☐ 8:1-35	☐ 9:1-27	☐ 10:1-43	☐ 11:1—12:24
31	☐ 13:1-33	☐ 14:1—15:63	☐ 16:1—18:28	☐ 19:1-51	☐ 20:1—21:45	☐ 22:1-34	☐ 23:1—24:33
32	☐ Judg 1:1-36	☐ 2:1-23	☐ 3:1-31	☐ 4:1-24	☐ 5:1-31	☐ 6:1-40	☐ 7:1-25
33	☐ 8:1-35	☐ 9:1-57	☐ 10:1—11:40	☐ 12:1—13:25	☐ 14:1—15:20	☐ 16:1-31	☐ 17:1—18:31
34	☐ 19:1-30	☐ 20:1-48	☐ 21:1-25	☐ Ruth 1:1-22	☐ 2:1-23	☐ 3:1-18	☐ 4:1-22
35	☐ 1 Sam 1:1-28	☐ 2:1-36	☐ 3:1—4:22	☐ 5:1—6:21	☐ 7:1—8:22	☐ 9:1-27	☐ 10:1—11:15
36	☐ 12:1—13:23	☐ 14:1-52	☐ 15:1-35	☐ 16:1-23	☐ 17:1-58	☐ 18:1-30	☐ 19:1-24
37	☐ 20:1-42	☐ 21:1—22:23	☐ 23:1—24:22	☐ 25:1-44	☐ 26:1-25	☐ 27:1—28:25	☐ 29:1—30:31
38	☐ 31:1-13	☐ 2 Sam 1:1-27	☐ 2:1-32	☐ 3:1-39	☐ 4:1—5:25	☐ 6:1-23	☐ 7:1-29
39	☐ 8:1—9:13	☐ 10:1—11:27	☐ 12:1-31	☐ 13:1-39	☐ 14:1-33	☐ 15:1—16:23	☐ 17:1—18:33
40	☐ 19:1-43	☐ 20:1—21:22	☐ 22:1-51	☐ 23:1-39	☐ 24:1-25	☐ 1 Kings 1:1-19	☐ 1:20-53
41	☐ 2:1-46	☐ 3:1-28	☐ 4:1-34	☐ 5:1—6:38	☐ 7:1-22	☐ 7:23-51	☐ 8:1-36
42	☐ 8:37-66	☐ 9:1-28	☐ 10:1-29	☐ 11:1-43	☐ 12:1-33	☐ 13:1-34	☐ 14:1-31
43	☐ 15:1-34	☐ 16:1—17:24	☐ 18:1-46	☐ 19:1-21	☐ 20:1-43	☐ 21:1—22:53	☐ 2 Kings 1:1-18
44	☐ 2:1—3:27	☐ 4:1-44	☐ 5:1—6:33	☐ 7:1-20	☐ 8:1-29	☐ 9:1-37	☐ 10:1-36
45	☐ 11:1—12:21	☐ 13:1—14:29	☐ 15:1-38	☐ 16:1-20	☐ 17:1-41	☐ 18:1-37	☐ 19:1-37
46	☐ 20:1—21:26	☐ 22:1-20	☐ 23:1-37	☐ 24:1—25:30	☐ 1 Chron 1:1-54	☐ 2:1—3:24	☐ 4:1—5:26
47	☐ 6:1-81	☐ 7:1-40	☐ 8:1-40	☐ 9:1-44	☐ 10:1—11:47	☐ 12:1-40	☐ 13:1—14:17
48	☐ 15:1—16:43	☐ 17:1-27	☐ 18:1—19:19	☐ 20:1—21:30	☐ 22:1—23:32	☐ 24:1—25:31	☐ 26:1-32
49	☐ 27:1-34	☐ 28:1—29:30	☐ 2 Chron 1:1-17	☐ 2:1—3:17	☐ 4:1—5:14	☐ 6:1-42	☐ 7:1—8:18
50	☐ 9:1—10:19	☐ 11:1—12:16	☐ 13:1—15:19	☐ 16:1—17:19	☐ 18:1—19:11	☐ 20:1-37	☐ 21:1—22:12
51	☐ 23:1—24:27	☐ 25:1—26:23	☐ 27:1—28:27	☐ 29:1-36	☐ 30:1—31:21	☐ 32:1-33	☐ 33:1—34:33
52	☐ 35:1—36:23	☐ Ezra 1:1-11	☐ 2:1-70	☐ 3:1—4:24	☐ 5:1—6:22	☐ 7:1-28	☐ 8:1-36

Reading Schedule for the Recovery Version of the Old Testament with Footnotes

Wk.	Lord's Day	Monday	Tuesday	Wednesday	Thursday	Friday	Saturday
53	9:1—10:44	Neh 1:1-11	2:1—3:32	4:1—5:19	6:1-19	7:1-73	8:1-18
54	9:1-20	9:21-38	10:1—11:36	12:1-47	13:1-31	Esth 1:1-22	2:1—3:15
55	4:1—5:14	6:1—7:10	8:1-17	9:1—10:3	Job 1:1-22	2:1—3:26	4:1—5:27
56	6:1—7:21	8:1—9:35	10:1—11:20	12:1—13:28	14:1—15:35	16:1—17:16	18:1—19:29
57	20:1—21:34	22:1—23:17	24:1—25:6	26:1—27:23	28:1—29:25	30:1—31:40	32:1—33:33
58	34:1—35:16	36:1-33	37:1-24	38:1-41	39:1-30	40:1-24	41:1-34
59	42:1-17	Psa 1:1-6	2:1—3:8	4:1—6:10	7:1—8:9	9:1—10:18	11:1—15:5
60	16:1—17:15	18:1-50	19:1—21:13	22:1-31	23:1—24:10	25:1—27:14	28:1—30:12
61	31:1—32:11	33:1—34:22	35:1—36:12	37:1-40	38:1—39:13	40:1—41:13	42:1—43:5
62	44:1-26	45:1-17	46:1—48:14	49:1—50:23	51:1—52:9	53:1—55:23	56:1—58:11
63	59:1—61:8	62:1—64:10	65:1—67:7	68:1-35	69:1—70:5	71:1—72:20	73:1—74:23
64	75:1—77:20	78:1-72	79:1—81:16	82:1—84:12	85:1—87:7	88:1—89:52	90:1—91:16
65	92:1—94:23	95:1—97:12	98:1—101:8	102:1—103:22	104:1—105:45	106:1-48	107:1-43
66	108:1—109:31	110:1—112:10	113:1—115:18	116:1—118:29	119:1-32	119:33-72	119:73-120
67	119:121-176	120:1—124:8	125:1—128:6	129:1—132:18	133:1—135:21	136:1—138:8	139:1—140:13
68	141:1—144:15	145:1—147:20	148:1—150:6	Prov 1:1-33	2:1—3:35	4:1—5:23	6:1-35
69	7:1—8:36	9:1—10:32	11:1—12:28	13:1—14:35	15:1-33	16:1-33	17:1-28
70	18:1-24	19:1—20:30	21:1—22:29	23:1-35	24:1—25:28	26:1—27:27	28:1—29:27
71	30:1-33	31:1-31	Eccl 1:1-18	2:1—3:22	4:1—5:20	6:1—7:29	8:1—9:18
72	10:1—11:10	12:1-14	S.S 1:1-8	1:9-17	2:1-17	3:1-11	4:1-8
73	4:9-16	5:1-16	6:1-13	7:1-13	8:1-14	Isa 1:1-11	1:12-31
74	2:1-22	3:1-26	4:1-6	5:1-30	6:1-13	7:1-25	8:1-22
75	9:1-21	10:1-34	11:1—12:6	13:1-22	14:1-14	14:15-32	15:1—16:14
76	17:1—18:7	19:1-25	20:1—21:17	22:1-25	23:1-18	24:1-23	25:1-12
77	26:1-21	27:1-13	28:1-29	29:1-24	30:1-33	31:1—32:20	33:1-24
78	34:1-17	35:1-10	36:1-22	37:1-38	38:1—39:8	40:1-31	41:1-29

Reading Schedule for the Recovery Version of the Old Testament with Footnotes

Wk.	Lord's Day	Monday	Tuesday	Wednesday	Thursday	Friday	Saturday
79	☐ 42:1-25	☐ 43:1-28	☐ 44:1-28	☐ 45:1-25	☐ 46:1-13	☐ 47:1-15	☐ 48:1-22
80	☐ 49:1-13	☐ 49:14-26	☐ 50:1—51:23	☐ 52:1-15	☐ 53:1-12	☐ 54:1-17	☐ 55:1-13
81	☐ 56:1-12	☐ 57:1-21	☐ 58:1-14	☐ 59:1-21	☐ 60:1-22	☐ 61:1-11	☐ 62:1-12
82	☐ 63:1-19	☐ 64:1-12	☐ 65:1-25	☐ 66:1-24	☐ Jer 1:1-19	☐ 2:1-19	☐ 2:20-37
83	☐ 3:1-25	☐ 4:1-31	☐ 5:1-31	☐ 6:1-30	☐ 7:1-34	☐ 8:1-22	☐ 9:1-26
84	☐ 10:1-25	☐ 11:1—12:17	☐ 13:1-27	☐ 14:1-22	☐ 15:1-21	☐ 16:1—17:27	☐ 18:1-23
85	☐ 19:1—20:18	☐ 21:1—22:30	☐ 23:1-40	☐ 24:1—25:38	☐ 26:1—27:22	☐ 28:1—29:32	☐ 30:1-24
86	☐ 31:1-23	☐ 31:24-40	☐ 32:1-44	☐ 33:1-26	☐ 34:1-22	☐ 35:1-19	☐ 36:1-32
87	☐ 37:1-21	☐ 38:1-28	☐ 39:1—40:16	☐ 41:1—42:22	☐ 43:1—44:30	☐ 45:1—46:28	☐ 47:1—48:16
88	☐ 48:17-47	☐ 49:1-22	☐ 49:23-39	☐ 50:1-27	☐ 50:28-46	☐ 51:1-27	☐ 51:28-64
89	☐ 52:1-34	☐ Lam 1:1-22	☐ 2:1-22	☐ 3:1-39	☐ 3:40-66	☐ 4:1-22	☐ 5:1-22
90	☐ Ezek 1:1-14	☐ 1:15-28	☐ 2:1—3:27	☐ 4:1—5:17	☐ 6:1—7:27	☐ 8:1—9:11	☐ 10:1—11:25
91	☐ 12:1—13:23	☐ 14:1—15:8	☐ 16:1-63	☐ 17:1—18:32	☐ 19:1-14	☐ 20:1-49	☐ 21:1-32
92	☐ 22:1-31	☐ 23:1-49	☐ 24:1-27	☐ 25:1—26:21	☐ 27:1-36	☐ 28:1-26	☐ 29:1—30:26
93	☐ 31:1—32:32	☐ 33:1-33	☐ 34:1-31	☐ 35:1—36:21	☐ 36:22-38	☐ 37:1-28	☐ 38:1—39:29
94	☐ 40:1-27	☐ 40:28-49	☐ 41:1-26	☐ 42:1—43:27	☐ 44:1-31	☐ 45:1-25	☐ 46:1-24
95	☐ 47:1-23	☐ 48:1-35	☐ Dan 1:1-21	☐ 2:1-30	☐ 2:31-49	☐ 3:1-30	☐ 4:1-37
96	☐ 5:1-31	☐ 6:1-28	☐ 7:1-12	☐ 7:13-28	☐ 8:1-27	☐ 9:1-27	☐ 10:1-21
97	☐ 11:1-22	☐ 11:23-45	☐ 12:1-13	☐ Hosea 1:1-11	☐ 2:1-23	☐ 3:1—4:19	☐ 5:1-15
98	☐ 6:1-11	☐ 7:1-16	☐ 8:1-14	☐ 9:1-17	☐ 10:1-15	☐ 11:1-12	☐ 12:1-14
99	☐ 13:1—14:9	☐ Joel 1:1-20	☐ 2:1-16	☐ 2:17-32	☐ 3:1-21	☐ Amos 1:1-15	☐ 2:1-16
100	☐ 3:1-15	☐ 4:1—5:27	☐ 6:1—7:17	☐ 8:1—9:15	☐ Obad 1-21	☐ Jonah 1:1-17	☐ 2:1—4:11
101	☐ Micah 1:1-16	☐ 2:1—3:12	☐ 4:1—5:15	☐ 6:1—7:20	☐ Nahum 1:1-15	☐ 2:1—3:19	☐ Hab 1:1-17
102	☐ 2:1-20	☐ 3:1-19	☐ Zeph 1:1-18	☐ 2:1-15	☐ 3:1-20	☐ Hag 1:1-15	☐ 2:1-23
103	☐ Zech 1:1-21	☐ 2:1-13	☐ 3:1-10	☐ 4:1-14	☐ 5:1—6:15	☐ 7:1—8:23	☐ 9:1-17
104	☐ 10:1—11:17	☐ 12:1—13:9	☐ 14:1-21	☐ Mal 1:1-14	☐ 2:1-17	☐ 3:1-18	☐ 4:1-6

Reading Schedule for the Recovery Version of the New Testament with Footnotes

Wk.	Lord's Day	Monday	Tuesday	Wednesday	Thursday	Friday	Saturday
1	☐ Matt 1:1-2	☐ 1:3-7	☐ 1:8-17	☐ 1:18-25	☐ 2:1-23	☐ 3:1-6	☐ 3:7-17
2	☐ 4:1-11	☐ 4:12-25	☐ 5:1-4	☐ 5:5-12	☐ 5:13-20	☐ 5:21-26	☐ 5:27-48
3	☐ 6:1-8	☐ 6:9-18	☐ 6:19-34	☐ 7:1-12	☐ 7:13-29	☐ 8:1-13	☐ 8:14-22
4	☐ 8:23-34	☐ 9:1-13	☐ 9:14-17	☐ 9:18-34	☐ 9:35—10:5	☐ 10:6-25	☐ 10:26-42
5	☐ 11:1-15	☐ 11:16-30	☐ 12:1-14	☐ 12:15-32	☐ 12:33-42	☐ 12:43—13:2	☐ 13:3-12
6	☐ 13:13-30	☐ 13:31-43	☐ 13:44-58	☐ 14:1-13	☐ 14:14-21	☐ 14:22-36	☐ 15:1-20
7	☐ 15:21-31	☐ 15:32-39	☐ 16:1-12	☐ 16:13-20	☐ 16:21-28	☐ 17:1-13	☐ 17:14-27
8	☐ 18:1-14	☐ 18:15-22	☐ 18:23-35	☐ 19:1-15	☐ 19:16-30	☐ 20:1-16	☐ 20:17-34
9	☐ 21:1-11	☐ 21:12-22	☐ 21:23-32	☐ 21:33-46	☐ 22:1-22	☐ 22:23-33	☐ 22:34-46
10	☐ 23:1-12	☐ 23:13-39	☐ 24:1-14	☐ 24:15-31	☐ 24:32-51	☐ 25:1-13	☐ 25:14-30
11	☐ 25:31-46	☐ 26:1-16	☐ 26:17-35	☐ 26:36-46	☐ 26:47-64	☐ 26:65-75	☐ 27:1-26
12	☐ 27:27-44	☐ 27:45-56	☐ 27:57—28:15	☐ 28:16-20	☐ Mark 1:1	☐ 1:2-6	☐ 1:7-13
13	☐ 1:14-28	☐ 1:29-45	☐ 2:1-12	☐ 2:13-28	☐ 3:1-19	☐ 3:20-35	☐ 4:1-25
14	☐ 4:26-41	☐ 5:1-20	☐ 5:21-43	☐ 6:1-29	☐ 6:30-56	☐ 7:1-23	☐ 7:24-37
15	☐ 8:1-26	☐ 8:27—9:1	☐ 9:2-29	☐ 9:30-50	☐ 10:1-16	☐ 10:17-34	☐ 10:35-52
16	☐ 11:1-16	☐ 11:17-33	☐ 12:1-27	☐ 12:28-44	☐ 13:1-13	☐ 13:14-37	☐ 14:1-26
17	☐ 14:27-52	☐ 14:53-72	☐ 15:1-15	☐ 15:16-47	☐ 16:1-8	☐ 16:9-20	☐ Luke 1:1-4
18	☐ 1:5-25	☐ 1:26-46	☐ 1:47-56	☐ 1:57-80	☐ 2:1-8	☐ 2:9-20	☐ 2:21-39
19	☐ 2:40-52	☐ 3:1-20	☐ 3:21-38	☐ 4:1-13	☐ 4:14-30	☐ 4:31-44	☐ 5:1-26
20	☐ 5:27—6:16	☐ 6:17-38	☐ 6:39-49	☐ 7:1-17	☐ 7:18-23	☐ 7:24-35	☐ 7:36-50
21	☐ 8:1-15	☐ 8:16-25	☐ 8:26-39	☐ 8:40-56	☐ 9:1-17	☐ 9:18-26	☐ 9:27-36
22	☐ 9:37-50	☐ 9:51-62	☐ 10:1-11	☐ 10:12-24	☐ 10:25-37	☐ 10:38-42	☐ 11:1-13
23	☐ 11:14-26	☐ 11:27-36	☐ 11:37-54	☐ 12:1-12	☐ 12:13-21	☐ 12:22-34	☐ 12:35-48
24	☐ 12:49-59	☐ 13:1-9	☐ 13:10-17	☐ 13:18-30	☐ 13:31—14:6	☐ 14:7-14	☐ 14:15-24
25	☐ 14:25-35	☐ 15:1-10	☐ 15:11-21	☐ 15:22-32	☐ 16:1-13	☐ 16:14-22	☐ 16:23-31
26	☐ 17:1-19	☐ 17:20-37	☐ 18:1-14	☐ 18:15-30	☐ 18:31-43	☐ 19:1-10	☐ 19:11-27

Reading Schedule for the Recovery Version of the New Testament with Footnotes

Wk.	Lord's Day	Monday	Tuesday	Wednesday	Thursday	Friday	Saturday
27	Luke 19:28-48	20:1-19	20:20-38	20:39—21:4	21:5-27	21:28-38	22:1-20
28	22:21-38	22:39-54	22:55-71	23:1-43	23:44-56	24:1-12	24:13-35
29	24:36-53	John 1:1-13	1:14-18	1:19-34	1:35-51	2:1-11	2:12-22
30	2:23—3:13	3:14-21	3:22-36	4:1-14	4:15-26	4:27-42	4:43-54
31	5:1-16	5:17-30	5:31-47	6:1-15	6:16-31	6:32-51	6:52-71
32	7:1-9	7:10-24	7:25-36	7:37-52	7:53—8:11	8:12-27	8:28-44
33	8:45-59	9:1-13	9:14-34	9:35—10:9	10:10-30	10:31—11:4	11:5-22
34	11:23-40	11:41-57	12:1-11	12:12-24	12:25-36	12:37-50	13:1-11
35	13:12-30	13:31-38	14:1-6	14:7-20	14:21-31	15:1-11	15:12-27
36	16:1-15	16:16-33	17:1-5	17:6-13	17:14-24	17:25—18:11	18:12-27
37	18:28-40	19:1-16	19:17-30	19:31-42	20:1-13	20:14-18	20:19-22
38	20:23-31	21:1-14	21:15-22	21:23-25	Acts 1:1-8	1:9-14	1:15-26
39	2:1-13	2:14-21	2:22-36	2:37-41	2:42-47	3:1-18	3:19—4:22
40	4:23-37	5:1-16	5:17-32	5:33-42	6:1—7:1	7:2-29	7:30-60
41	8:1-13	8:14-25	8:26-40	9:1-19	9:20-43	10:1-16	10:17-33
42	10:34-48	11:1-18	11:19-30	12:1-25	13:1-12	13:13-43	13:44—14:5
43	14:6-28	15:1-12	15:13-34	15:35—16:5	16:6-18	16:19-40	17:1-18
44	17:19-34	18:1-17	18:18-28	19:1-20	19:21-41	20:1-12	20:13-38
45	21:1-14	21:15-26	21:27-40	22:1-21	22:22-29	22:30—23:11	23:12-15
46	23:16-30	23:31—24:21	24:22—25:5	25:6-27	26:1-13	26:14-32	27:1-26
47	27:27—28:10	28:11-22	28:23-31	Rom 1:1-2	1:3-7	1:8-17	1:18-25
48	1:26—2:10	2:11-29	3:1-20	3:21-31	4:1-12	4:13-25	5:1-11
49	5:12-17	5:18—6:5	6:6-11	6:12-23	7:1-12	7:13-25	8:1-2
50	8:3-6	8:7-13	8:14-25	8:26-39	9:1-18	9:19—10:3	10:4-15
51	10:16—11:10	11:11-22	11:23-36	12:1-3	12:4-21	13:1-14	14:1-12
52	14:13-23	15:1-13	15:14-33	16:1-5	16:6-24	16:25-27	1 Cor 1:1-4

Reading Schedule for the Recovery Version of the New Testament with Footnotes

Wk.	Lord's Day	Monday	Tuesday	Wednesday	Thursday	Friday	Saturday
53	1 Cor 1:5-9	1:10-17	1:18-31	2:1-5	2:6-10	2:11-16	3:1-9
54	3:10-13	3:14-23	4:1-9	4:10-21	5:1-13	6:1-11	6:12-20
55	7:1-16	7:17-24	7:25-40	8:1-13	9:1-15	9:16-27	10:1-4
56	10:5-13	10:14-33	11:1-6	11:7-16	11:17-26	11:27-34	12:1-11
57	12:12-22	12:23-31	13:1-13	14:1-12	14:13-25	14:26-33	14:34-40
58	15:1-19	15:20-28	15:29-34	15:35-49	15:50-58	16:1-9	16:10-24
59	2 Cor 1:1-4	1:5-14	1:15-22	1:23—2:11	2:12-17	3:1-6	3:7-11
60	3:12-18	4:1-6	4:7-12	4:13-18	5:1-8	5:9-15	5:16-21
61	6:1-13	6:14—7:4	7:5-16	8:1-15	8:16-24	9:1-15	10:1-6
62	10:7-18	11:1-15	11:16-33	12:1-10	12:11-21	13:1-10	13:11-14
63	Gal 1:1-5	1:6-14	1:15-24	2:1-13	2:14-21	3:1-4	3:5-14
64	3:15-22	3:23-29	4:1-7	4:8-20	4:21-31	5:1-12	5:13-21
65	5:22-26	6:1-10	6:11-15	6:16-18	Eph 1:1-3	1:4-6	1:7-10
66	1:11-14	1:15-18	1:19-23	2:1-5	2:6-10	2:11-14	2:15-18
67	2:19-22	3:1-7	3:8-13	3:14-18	3:19-21	4:1-4	4:5-10
68	4:11-16	4:17-24	4:25-32	5:1-10	5:11-21	5:22-26	5:27-33
69	6:1-9	6:10-14	6:15-18	6:19-24	Phil 1:1-7	1:8-18	1:19-26
70	1:27—2:4	2:5-11	2:12-16	2:17-30	3:1-6	3:7-11	3:12-16
71	3:17-21	4:1-9	4:10-23	Col 1:1-8	1:9-13	1:14-23	1:24-29
72	2:1-7	2:8-15	2:16-23	3:1-4	3:5-15	3:16-25	4:1-18
73	1 Thes 1:1-3	1:4-10	2:1-12	2:13—3:5	3:6-13	4:1-10	4:11—5:11
74	5:12-28	2 Thes 1:1-12	2:1-17	3:1-18	1 Tim 1:1-2	1:3-4	1:5-14
75	1:15-20	2:1-7	2:8-15	3:1-13	3:14—4:5	4:6-16	5:1-25
76	6:1-10	6:11-21	2 Tim 1:1-10	1:11-18	2:1-15	2:16-26	3:1-13
77	3:14—4:8	4:9-22	Titus 1:1-4	1:5-16	2:1-15	3:1-8	3:9-15
78	Philem 1:1-11	1:12-25	Heb 1:1-2	1:3-5	1:6-14	2:1-9	2:10-18